THE TET OFFENSIVE

VIETNAM
America in the War Years

Series Editor
David L. Anderson
California State University Monterey Bay

The Vietnam War and the tumultuous internal upheavals in America that coincided with it marked a watershed era in U.S. history. These events profoundly challenged America's heroic self-image. During the 1950s the United States defined Southeast Asia as an area of vital strategic importance. In the 1960s this view produced a costly American military campaign that continued into the early 1970s. The Vietnam War was the nation's longest war and ended with an unprecedented U.S. failure to achieve its stated objectives. Simultaneous with this frustrating military intervention and the domestic debate that it produced were other tensions created by student activism on campuses, the black struggle for civil rights, and the women's liberation movement. The books in this series explore the complex and controversial issues of the period from the mid-1950s to the mid-1970s in brief and engaging volumes. To facilitate continued and informed debate on these contested subjects, each book examines a military, political, or diplomatic issue; the role of a key individual; or one of the domestic changes in America during the war.

Volumes Published

THE TET OFFENSIVE

Politics, War, and Public Opinion

David F. Schmitz

ROWMAN & LITTLEFIELD PUBLISHERS, INC.
Lanham • Boulder • New York • Toronto • Oxford

ROWMAN & LITTLEFIELD PUBLISHERS, INC.

Published in the United States of America
by Rowman & Littlefield Publishers, Inc.
A wholly owned subsidary of The Rowman & Littlefield Publishing Group, Inc.
4501 Forbes Boulevard, Suite 200, Lanham, Maryland 20706
www.rowmanlittlefield.com

PO Box 317
Oxford
OX2 9RU, UK

British Library Cataloguing in Publication Information Available

Library of Congress Cataloging-in-Publication Data

Schmitz, David F.
 The Tet Offensive : politics, war, and public opinion / David F. Schmitz.
  p. cm.—(Vietnam—America in the war years)
 Includes bibliographical references and index.
  ISBN 0-7425-4485-0 (cloth : alk. paper)—ISBN 0-7425-4486-9 (pbk. : alk. paper)
 I. Tet Offensive, 1968. 2. Vietnamese Conflict, 1961–1975—Public opinion.
3. Vietnamese Conflict, 1961–1975—United States. 4. Public opinion—United
States. I. Title. II. Series: Vietnam—America in the war years (Unnumbered)
DS557.8.T4S39 2005
959.704'334—dc22   2005010736

Printed in the United States of America

∞™ The paper used in this publication meets the minimum requirements of
American National Standard for Information Sciences—Permanence of Paper for
Printed Library Materials, ANSI/NISO Z39.48-1992.

To Polly

CONTENTS

ABBREVIATIONS

ARVN	Army of the Republic of Vietnam
AWF	Papers as President of the United States, 1953–1961 (Ann Whitman Files), Dwight D. Eisenhower Papers, Dwight D. Eisenhower Presidential Library
CCP	Chinese Communist Party
CIA	Central Intelligence Agency
CORDS	Civilian Operations and Revolutionary Development Support Program
CPI	Consumer Price Index
DDEL	Dwight D. Eisenhower Presidential Library
DH Series	Dulles-Herter Series, Dwight D. Eisenhower Presidential Library
DMZ	Demilitarized Zone
FRUS	*Foreign Relations of the United States*
FY	Fiscal Year
GVN	Government of South Vietnam
HSTL	Harry S. Truman Presidential Library
ISA	Office of International Security Affairs, Department of Defense
JCS	Joint Chiefs of Staff

JFKL	John F. Kennedy Presidential Library
KIA	Killed in Action
LBJL	Lyndon B. Johnson Presidential Library
MACV	Military Assistance Command, Vietnam
NATO	North Atlantic Treaty Organization
NIE	National Intelligence Estimate
NLF	National Liberation Front
NSC	National Security Council
NSF	National Security File
NSF: CO	National Security Files: Country
NVA	North Vietnamese Army
NVN	North Vietnam
POW	Prisoners of War
SFRC	Senate Foreign Relations Committee
SVN	South Vietnam
VC	Viet Cong (Vietnamese Communists)
WHCF	White House Central File

ACKNOWLEDGMENTS

I THANK DAVID ANDERSON, THE SERIES EDITOR, AND Laura Roberts Gottlieb, for including my book in this series. David provided guidance on the goals of the series, probing questions, good suggestions, and support throughout the process. His editorial skill brought greater clarity and precision to a number of points. It has been a pleasure to work with both of them.

Whitman College provided generous support that allowed me to travel to archives to conduct research. Through the Lewis B. Perry Summer Research Scholarship Program I was able to employ Erin Gettling as a research assistant. She assisted me in locating documents at the Lyndon B. Johnson Presidential Library and on numerous other tasks. Erin and Vanessa Walker read the entire manuscript and made excellent suggestions for improvements. Jillian Huber helped with locating documents and polling information.

My colleagues in the History Department at Whitman College graciously read chapter 4 during one of our First Friday sessions and helped me sharpen my analysis. My first research on the Vietnam War was done under the guidance of Lloyd Gardner and his teaching and scholarship remain essential to my work. T. Christopher Jespersen and Fred Logevall discussed my ideas on this book with me on numerous occasions and generously shared their vast knowledge on the Vietnam War.

The archivists at the Lyndon B. Johnson Presidential Library deserve special notice for their excellent and professional assistance. In particular, John Wilson provided me with a comprehensive guide to the documents on Tet while pointing me to collections that I might have missed. Kyla Wilson graciously helped me find the photographs for this book, and Michael McDonald made Johnson's sand table map of Khe Sanh available for me to photograph. Back home, Kathy Guizar provided expert assistance in preparing the photographs for publication.

I have learned a great deal in the past twenty years from all of my students at Whitman College who have taken my course on the Vietnam War. I want to thank them for always asking good questions and inspiring me to write this book. My children Nicole and Kincaid have provided other inspirations to write about such topics.

Finally, I dedicate this book to my wife Polly. Whether visiting sites together in Vietnam or discussing the Tet Offensive in Walla Walla, she has contributed to this work in more ways than I can count. In all ways, she enriches my life.

INTRODUCTION

The Tet Offensive, which began on January 30, 1968, is arguably the most important event of the Vietnam War. The largest set of battles in the war up to that point, and the first to be fought in the cities of South Vietnam, the Tet Offensive is significant in the military aspects of the fighting, but its greater importance is its political and psychological impact in the United States and, in particular, inside the Johnson administration. Tet changed the nature of the debate about the war, enlarged the credibility gap between the administration's explanations of events in Vietnam and the public's understanding of the war, created an economic crisis at home, and bolstered the presidential aspirations of antiwar candidates Senators Eugene McCarthy and Robert Kennedy. In the process, it forced a reevaluation of American policy by senior administration officials that culminated in President Lyndon Johnson's decisions to cap the American escalation of the war, impose a partial bombing halt on the air war against North Vietnam, seek negotiations with Hanoi, and withdraw from the 1968 presidential race.

As one of the key moments of the Vietnam War and an event of great military, political, and psychological significance, the Tet Offensive remains one of the most controversial aspects of the war. Interpretations of it are central to the debates over the reasons for the eventual American withdrawal from Vietnam and failure to maintain a noncommunist government in Saigon. Supporters of the Vietnam War claim that the Tet Offensive was a tremendous military victory for the United States that was turned into a political defeat in the United States due to biased news coverage, particularly on television, that distorted the event, created an appearance of defeat instead of victory, and caused a panic at home and the collapse of public support for the war. This television thesis has been challenged by critics of the war who point to Tet as proof that the United States had committed a tragic mistake in going to war in Vietnam, and that the fighting was a bloody stalemate that demonstrated that Washington could not create a viable government in Saigon or win the war within a reasonable time period or at acceptable costs.

Surprisingly, given the pivotal nature of the Tet Offensive and the debates surrounding it, there are no scholarly monographs that examine the whole event. Don Oberdorfer's *TET!*, published in 1971, provides a journalistic account of the story and is an excellent source, but it lacks an historical perspective on its meaning.[1] There are also a number of excellent chapters on the Tet Offensive within larger studies on the Vietnam War and specialized studies of particular aspects of the offensive.[2] Using the available primary documents and the latest scholarship on the war, this study examines the military, political, and economic aspects of the Tet Offensive to demonstrate that the Tet Offensive represented a defeat for the United States and its policy in Vietnam and that the media coverage of Tet did not sway American opinion or cause the Johnson administration to change its policy.

The claim of media bias, besides being incorrect, places the focus of the discussion in the wrong place as there was no sudden change of opinion on the war by the American people. Rather, the Tet Offensive was the decisive moment in the Vietnam War due to its impact on senior officials in the Johnson administration and elite opinion that brought about Johnson's dramatic decisions and change in policy. Their views on the war, most notably those of Secretary of Defense Clark Clifford, former National Security Advisor McGeorge Bundy, and former Secretary of State and architect of the Truman Doctrine and containment Dean Acheson, changed dramatically. Prior to Tet, they saw the U.S. commitment and escalation as necessary policies to uphold containment and demonstrate American credibility and resolve through a limited war that would deter communist aggression without escalating into a global conflict. After Tet, there was an opening for dissenting views, negative reports, and alternative opinions to be heard that led these policy makers to conclude that the war was an unwinnable stalemate and that a change of policy was necessary to extract the United States from the political and economic crises the Vietnam War had created at home. The American goal of maintaining a noncommunist government in Saigon could not be achieved by American military action.

To say that the Tet Offensive was a defeat for the United States is not to dismiss the enormous losses suffered by the enemy in the early months of 1968, or the success of American forces in retaking all of the cities in South Vietnam. These military achievements were a victory only in the narrowest sense of military targets held or lost. Battles in wars, however, are not fought in isolation. They are simultaneously military, political, and diplomatic actions taken in an effort to achieve the ultimate goal of defeating the enemy. American forces could prevent the overthrow of the Saigon government, inflict a high level of casualties, and create enormous destruction. But they could not create a stable, legitimate government in South Vietnam or destroy the enemy's capacity and will to fight. In the aftermath of the Tet Offensive, the costs of maintaining the stalemate, in the estimation of the Johnson administration, were increasing with no end in sight and the continued escalation of the war had to stop. Thus, the American policy of a limited war of attrition suffered a defeat during the Tet Offensive.

In order to fully understand the profound impact of the Tet Offensive on a generation of U.S. strategic doctrine, it must be situated in the context of American policy and the state of the war up to 1968. The first chapter, therefore, provides an overview of the Cold War policy of containment, the logic and rationale for American involvement in Vietnam, and decision to escalate the American commitment in 1965. Chapter 2 examines the state of the war by 1967, the nature of the domestic debate over Vietnam, the first meeting of the so-called Wise Men, the Johnson administration's conclusion in the fall 1967 that it was winning the war, and the subsequent public relations effort to rally support for the war and convince the American people that the end was in sight. The third chapter discusses the attacks on the cities, the varied and differing explanations and understandings of the offensive, and its impact on the United States and the Johnson administration through the end of February 1968. The following chapter takes up the critical events and decisions made during March 1968, culminating in President Johnson's March 31, 1968, speech to the nation that announced his change of policy and decision not to run for reelection. In conclusion, chapter 5 examines the two central debates about Tet, concerning the claim that the media's coverage of the offensive turned public opinion against that war and the question of a military victory, to demonstrate their inaccuracy and explain why the Tet Offensive was the decisive moment in the war.

NOTES

1. Don Oberdorfer, *TET!* (New York: Avon Books, 1971).

2. See the bibliographic essay for these sources.

Chapter One

THE AMERICAN ROAD TO VIETNAM

T HE END OF WORLD WAR II MARKED THE BEGINNING
of a new epoch in U.S. foreign policy in which the Vietnam
War and the Tet Offensive were key events. For Americans,
the postwar period promised a vindication of their nation's
values and institutions that they were sure other people
wanted to emulate and adopt. It was an article of faith that
non-Americans desired the things that the United States
represented and that the values of America were universal.
President Franklin D. Roosevelt declared that the war was
fought for the Four Freedoms—freedom of speech and religion, freedom from want and from fear—while simultaneously he criticized tyranny and colonialism and talked of the
expansion of American institutions to other parts of the
globe. In apparent agreement, the world's nations had joined
together in an antifascist coalition on the battlefield and
produced documents such as the Atlantic Charter and the
Charter of the United Nations that extolled the values of
human rights, self-determination, and freedom. To make
sure that these proclamations were not merely empty phrases
and symbolic gestures, Americans believed that they had to

1

take command of the world and accept the obligations of world leadership they had rejected in 1919. The spread of democracy would lessen, if not completely eliminate, the threat of another war and foster an international environment of free trade and cooperation led by the United States.

American officials were determined that the United States would seize its "second chance" to shape the postwar world. It was axiomatic to American internationalists that the United States should accept responsibility for postwar leadership and see to it that the world adopted American ideals of self-determination, free trade, arms limitation, and collective security to ensure postwar peace and prosperity. They agreed with Henry Luce, the publisher of *Time*, *Life*, and *Fortune*, that the failure of Americans to accept world leadership during the interwar period "had disastrous consequences for themselves and for all mankind," and that peace and prosperity could only be secured through the establishment of an "American Century." As Luce summarized the recent past, in 1919 the United States had missed "a golden opportunity . . . to assume the leadership of the world. . . . We did not understand that opportunity. [President Woodrow] Wilson mishandled it. We rejected it." The result was the Great Depression and a Second World War. To avoid a repeat of this past, the United States had to lead the world. "It is for America and America alone to determine," Luce opined, "whether a system of free enterprise—an economic order compatible with freedom and progress—shall or shall not prevail in this country. We know perfectly well that there is not the slightest chance of anything faintly resembling a free economic system prevailing in this country if it prevails nowhere else."[1] If the United States failed, economic disruption and political chaos would return, bringing another war and revolutionary upheaval.

Building on a long tradition of exceptionalism in American thought and a paternalistic racism that categorized all non-Western European people as inferior, and vulnerable to radical ideas and solutions, Luce argued that it was essential that the United States promote American ideals of freedom, justice, and opportunity to make sure they "spread throughout the world and do their mysterious work of lifting the life of mankind from the level of the beasts to what the Psalmist called a little lower than the angels." Luce declared: "America as the dynamic center of ever-widening spheres of enterprise, America as the training center of the skillful servants of mankind, America as the Good Samaritan, really believing again that it is more blessed to give than to receive, and America as the powerhouse of the ideals of Freedom and Justice—out of these elements surely can be fashioned a vision of the 20th Century to which we can and will devote ourselves." He concluded that "it is in this spirit that all of us are called, each to his own measure of capacity, and each in the widest horizon of his vision, to create the first great American Century."[2]

To America's postwar leaders, political and economic freedoms were interrelated, and American prosperity was dependent upon world economic recovery along liberal economic lines. Any restrictions of trade would lead, it was feared, to a repeat of the 1930s. President Harry S. Truman clearly outlined these views in early 1947. Going beyond Roosevelt's Four Freedoms, he declared in a speech at Baylor University that "peace, freedom, and world trade" are inseparable. "The grave lessons of the past have proved it." There was, Truman believed, "one thing that Americans value even more than peace. It is freedom. Freedom of worship—freedom of speech—freedom of enterprise." They, too, could not be separated. Americans' devotion to freedom of enterprise was contingent on the other two freedoms. It "has deeper roots than a desire to protect the profits of ownership. It is part and parcel of what we call American." If trends continued, however, the government would "shortly find itself in the business of allocating foreign goods among importers and foreign markets among exporters and telling every trader what he could buy or sell, and how much, and when, and where. This is precisely what we have been trying to get away from as rapidly as possible, ever since the war. It is not the American way. It is not the way to peace."[3]

The impediment to this American vision of peace and prosperity was the Soviet Union. From Washington, events in the Soviet-controlled areas of Europe came to be seen as hostile and aggressive actions against the interests of the United States. Clashes with the Soviet Union over the postwar government of Poland and German occupation policy convinced Truman by the end of 1945 that it was time to "stop babying the Soviets." He concluded that "unless Russia is faced with an iron fist and strong language, another war is in the making."[4]

The next year witnessed an increasing hostility toward the Soviet Union. The arrival of George Kennan's long telegram from Moscow in February 1946 served to provide coherence to the developing hard line against the Soviets. The Soviet Union, Kennan argued, had no legitimate security fears or grievances and, therefore, no justification for its actions in Eastern Europe. Rather, its leaders were motivated by a combination of traditional Russian desires to expand and Marxist ideology that taught there could be no cooperation with capitalist states. The "Kremlin's neurotic view of world affairs is traditional and instinctive Russian sense of insecurity." This meant that the United States was faced with "a political force committed fanatically to the belief that with US there can be no permanent *modus vivendi,* that it is desirable and necessary that the internal harmony of our society be disrupted, our traditional way of life be destroyed, the international authority of our state be broken, if Soviet power is to be secure." Given this, a policy of opposition and the containment of Soviet power was the only wise course to follow.[5]

On August 15, 1946, Truman endorsed a policy memorandum drawn up by his senior advisors that stated that the "time has come when we must decide that we shall resist with all means at our disposal any Soviet aggression." In particular, Turkey and the Turkish straits were identified as vital to American interests, and, therefore, military action might be necessary to keep them out of Russia's control.[6] That same month, Truman asked his special counsel in the White House, Clark Clifford, for a summary of all the agreements the Soviets had violated. The final report, prepared by Clifford's assistant George Elsey, went beyond the initial request and presented the president with an outline designed to provide a coherent outlook on relations with the Soviet Union. Drawing heavily upon Kennan, Clifford set out the problem of relations with Russia as an ideological challenge to Western liberalism that had to be met to insure the survival of freedom. Soviet foreign policy, he argued, was inherently expansive and the United States had to be prepared to meet it with military force.[7]

Problems seemed to be multiplying and from the White House it appeared that the source of all difficulties was Moscow. In Europe, economic recovery from the war was slow, food and other essential goods in short supply, communist parties, particularly in France and Italy, were gaining ground, and Soviet-installed governments in Eastern Europe were seemingly becoming entrenched. A new world crisis had arrived that demanded American resolve, and its focal point became the civil war that raged in Greece between the British-backed Royalist forces and the communist-led rebels.[8] The British announcement in February 1947 that they were pulling out of Greece spurred the Truman administration into action. Rather than viewing the conflict as a long-standing division within Greek society over the nature of its government and institutions, American policy makers interpreted it as part of a Soviet effort to expand. Undersecretary of State Dean Acheson told congressional leaders that the "Soviet Union was playing one of the greatest gambles in history at minimal cost." In an early version of the domino theory, he compared the situation in Greece to a barrel of apples infected by a rotten one. "The corruption of Greece would infect Iran and all to the east. It would also carry infection to Africa through Asia Minor and Egypt, and to Europe through Italy and France." The United States alone was "in a position to break up the play."[9]

In response, the president set out the Truman Doctrine in March 1947. The central theme of his speech was a global contest between two competing and incompatible ways of life: democracy and totalitarian communism. Democracy represented government "based upon the will of the majority" expressed through "free institutions, representative government, free elections, guarantees of individual liberty, freedom of speech and religion, and freedom from political oppression." Communism meant the "will of a minority forcibly imposed upon the majority. It relies on terror and oppression, a controlled press and radio, fixed elections, and the suppression of personal freedoms." The course of action was clear. "I believe," Truman declared, "that it must be the policy of the United States to support free peoples who are resisting attempted subjugation by armed minorities or by outside pressures."[10] The containment of communism was now the basis of American foreign policy.

A Manichean view of conflict between the United States and the Soviet Union forged a bipartisan consensus in support of containment. Americans agreed that the Soviet Union was inherently aggressive, expansive, and hostile to American interests, and that communism was a monolithic movement, emanating from Moscow and spreading to other parts of the world. There was no room for compromise or negotiation. The Soviets would take advantage of all sincere efforts at peace and only honor agreements when it was expedient. Moreover, communism was a totalitarian and evil system of government, an implacable foe of freedom and American values that sought nothing less than world conquest. Just as during World War II, the United States was faced by an enemy that was the antithesis of its values and a threat to its security and interests. Thus, the lesson learned less than a decade earlier at Munich, that you cannot appease an aggressor, was quickly applied by American policy makers. It was now a bipolar world where all international developments were seen as connected to the battle against communism and regional issues were submerged to the broader mandates of the emerging Cold War.

The Truman Doctrine and the adoption of the policy of containment manifested the optimism, faith, and confidence of post–World War II American society that any challenge could be overcome if the United States just had the will, resolve, and discipline to carry out its policy. To create the American Century, it would take adroit planning and leadership, matched with American intelligence, technology, money, and if necessary force, all things the United States appeared to have in abundance. The United States was on a winning streak. It had just overcome the

Great Depression and defeated Nazi Germany and Imperial Japan, and, because its cause was just, would triumph in the Cold War as well. Postwar prosperity confirmed for Americans the correctness of their institutions and policies and reinforced the notion that their values were universal and desired by all.

CONTAINMENT AND VIETNAM

While containment was successfully implemented in Europe, developments in East Asia appeared to the Truman administration to pose an equal, if not greater, threat to the free world. There, revolutionary nationalist movements, often headed by communists, were fighting against the restoration of Europe's colonial empires, while civil war between the American-supported Guomindang and the Chinese Communist Party (CCP) resumed in China. Containment, therefore, had to be globalized to meet the threat as anticommunism replaced anticolonialism as the paradigm for American foreign policy. The logic and rationale of containment led the United States into Vietnam first in support of France's efforts to reclaim its colonies in Southeast Asia and then to establish a new nation: South Vietnam. The Truman Doctrine and the rhetoric of a bipolar world created an ideological inflexibility in Washington that prevented any questioning of policy or new approaches. Vietnam was only important to the United States in terms of how it fit into the Cold War with communism, and this led American leaders to ignore the political realities of the nation and force Ho Chi Minh's nationalistic, anticolonial revolt into preexisting categories and roles as part of the expansion of the international communist movement.

Franklin Roosevelt had intended to place the French colony of Indochina under a United Nations trusteeship after the war. This, he believed, was necessary in order to allow for a proper transition and time to prepare the people for independence. As Roosevelt explained his policy to Secretary of State Cordell Hull in 1944, "it was perfectly true that I had, for over a year, expressed the opinion that Indo-China should not go back to France but that it should be administered by an international trusteeship. France has had the country—thirty million inhabitants for nearly one hundred years, and the people are worse off than they were at the beginning." As such, the case for taking the region away from France was "perfectly clear. . . . The people of Indo-China are entitled to something better than that."[11] This position was consistent with Roosevelt's view that the war in the Pacific was in large part the result of European imperialism and belief that colonialism in Asia was a dying system.[12] It also fit with his view that the Vietnamese, along with many other Asians, were not yet prepared for self-government. "With the Indo-Chinese," Roosevelt noted, "there is a feeling they ought to be independent but are not ready for it." They needed to be educated in the same manner that the Filipinos were. In that case, "it took fifty years for us to do it."[13]

Such paternalistic views ensured that Roosevelt and his immediate successors ruled out independence for Vietnam and provided the context for why the president began to back away from his position that France had to be kept out of Indochina in 1945. A combination of European pressure and the onset of the Cold War brought about an abandonment of this effort. The larger aim remained the same; the American "goal must be to help [colonial people] achieve independence." But when asked in March if he had "changed his ideas on French Indo-China," Roosevelt first answered no, then hesitated and added "if we can get the proper pledge from France to assume for herself the obligations of a trustee, then I would agree to France retaining these colonies with the proviso that independence was the ultimate goal."[14]

When Roosevelt died in April 1945, Truman inherited a policy in a state of flux. In the rush of events surrounding the end of the war in Europe, the decision to drop the atomic bombs, the end of the war in Japan, and deteriorating relations with the Soviet Union, French colonial policy and Vietnam did not command much of Truman's attention and energy during his first months in office. It was not surprising, therefore, that he took a cautious, and what must have appeared to him safe, course in deciding his policy. In May, after a review of policy by both the European and Far Eastern Divisions of the State Department, Truman approved the decision that the United States would allow a French return to Indochina and instructed the State Department to inform France that the United States did not question its sovereignty over Indochina.[15] It was expected that France would ensure that the region would be open to all for trade, and that it would work toward the establishment of a "democratic national or federal government to be run for and increasingly by the Indochinese themselves . . . so that within the foreseeable future Indochina may be fully self-governing and autonomous."[16] These were details to be worked out in the future. The immediate concern was stability. The door was opened for a French return with American support. American anticommunism and the logic of containment placed the United States in direct opposition to Ho Chi Minh's revolutionary nationalist movement, the Vietminh, and in

the position of supporting the first of a series of unpopular and non-democratic governments in Vietnam.

Before the French could secure their position, Ho Chi
Minh declared Vietnam's independence on September 2,
1945. Sporadic fighting between the Vietminh and the re-
turning French soon broke out, and after failed efforts at negotiations, the conflict escalated into full-scale war in late
1946. The American response was mixed. On the one hand,
the United States sought to aid its French ally and secure access to Indochina's raw materials and markets for France's
economic recovery. Unity in Europe was a high priority, and
there were few advocates of support for Ho. As Acheson
tersely noted in December 1946, officials had to "keep in
mind Ho's clear record as agent international communism."[17] On the other hand, the Truman administration did
not want to tie the U.S.'s reputation directly to European imperialism and refused to provide France the direct aid it requested. Washington still hoped that France would grant
more autonomy to the Vietnamese in order to undercut the
nationalist appeal of the Vietminh. But neither would it con-
demn French actions or prevent it from diverting aid sent to
Paris to the war effort in Southeast Asia.

In 1947, after the announcement of the Truman Doctrine, American policy began to gain more clarity. Secretary
of State George Marshall informed American diplomats in
France and Vietnam that the "key [to] our position is our
awareness that in respect [to] developments affecting position [of] Western democratic powers in southern Asia, we
[are] essentially in same boat as France." As the region
moves toward independence a "relaxation of European controls . . . could plunge new nations into violent discord . . .
[and] anti-Western Pan-Asiatic tendencies could become
dominant force, or Communists could capture control. We

consider as best safeguard against these eventualities a continued close association between newly-autonomous peoples and powers which have long been responsible for their
welfare." Specifically in terms of the fighting in Vietnam,
the United States believed that the Vietnamese "will for in-
definite period require French material and technical assistance and enlightened political guidance which can only be
provided by nation steeped like France in democratic tradition and confirmed in respect for human liberties and
worth of the individual."[18] Marshall wanted to be sure that
"we do not lose sight [of the] fact that Ho Chi Minh has
direct Communist connections and it should be obvious
that we are not interested in seeing colonial administrations
supplanted by philosophy and political organization emanating from and controlled by the Kremlin."[19] Thus, when
France established three associated states in Indochina
(Vietnam, Cambodia, and Laos) within the French Union
in 1949, placing Bao Dai at the head of the State of Vietnam, the Truman administration welcomed this move and
changed its position to open support of French policy.[20]

Now Secretary of State Dean Acheson bluntly eliminated any alternative position in May 1949. The "question
[of] whether Ho as much nationalist as Commie is irrele-
vant. All Stalinists in colonial areas are nationalists. With
achievement [of] natl aims (i.e. independence) their objective
necessarily becomes subordination [of] state to Commie
purposes and ruthless extermination not only [of] opposition groups but all elements suspected even slightest devia-
tion."[21] In 1950, the State Department outlined the options.
The choice was between supporting "Bao Dai (or a similar
anti-communist successor) or Ho Chi Minh (or a similar
communist successor); there is no other alternative." That
meant supporting the French or "face the extension of

Communism over the remainder of the continental area of Southeast Asia and, possibly, farther westward." It would be a "case of 'Penny wise, Pound foolish' to deny support to the French in Indochina."[22]

The Cold War turned hot in June 1950 with the outbreak of the Korean War. President Truman, invoking his doctrine, declared that the "Communists in the Kremlin are engaged in a monstrous conspiracy to stamp out freedom all over the world. If they were to succeed, the United States would be numbered among their principal victims." This demanded an American military response "to prevent a third world war." The United States, he stated, could not "sit idly by and await foreign conquest. . . . The best time to meet the threat is in the beginning." The lesson of the past was that "aggression anywhere in the world is a threat to peace everywhere in the world. When that aggression is supported by the cruel and selfish rulers of a powerful nation who are bent on conquest," it presented a clear danger to the United States. "If they had followed the right policies in the 1930's—if the free countries had acted together . . . in the beginning, when the aggression was small—there probably would have been no World War II."[23]

The strategy adopted during the Korean War was limited war. As President Truman explained the logic of this approach to those who criticized him for not expanding the war to include China, the United States was fighting to prevent "aggression from succeeding and bringing on a general war." By doing so, the United States was increasing the ability "of the whole free world to resist Communist aggression" so as to "make sure that the precious lives of our fighting men are not wasted; to see that the security of our country and the free world is not needlessly jeopardized; and to prevent a third world war." If the United States was to expand the war to China, "we would be running a grave risk of starting a general war. If that were to happen, we would have brought about the exact situation we are trying to prevent."[24]

The victory of the CCP in China in the fall of 1949 and the Korean War set off a political debate in the United States where the Truman administration was blamed for losing China to communism and helped fuel the rise of McCarthyism at home. Named after Senator Joseph McCarthy of Wisconsin, McCarthyism was the reckless hunt for domestic communists and attacks on those who purportedly protected them, leading to a fear by leaders of being seen as "soft" on communism and its containment. The corrupt, ineffective, and unpopular nature of the Guomindang government, the effectiveness of the CCP in recruiting Chinese peasants, and the extensive aid sent by the United States to China became secondary issues to the charge that the administration had failed to prevent the spread of communism and that Truman's State Department had communist sympathizers making policy for East Asia. These new realities of Cold War politics, and the inability to question the simple, bipolar worldview and visions of American omnipotence on which the McCarthyite charges were based, added urgency to the need to support the French effort in Vietnam.

On May 8, 1950, the United States formally recognized the government of Bao Dai as an independent state within the French Union and announced that it would send aid to his government, thereby joining the war in Vietnam. Acheson argued that this move was necessary because it would provide "encouragement to national aspirations under non-Communist leadership for peoples of colonial areas in Southeast Asia, the establishment of stable non-Communist governments in areas adjacent to Communist China" and support to an important European ally.[25] American interests were now best served by a direct association with the French in Vietnam. As far as the State Department could predict, "French forces appear to be the sole effective guarantee that communist forces will be resisted."[26] The first order of business was the defeat of communism. All other questions concerning full independence and the type of government in Vietnam would have to wait until the Vietminh were defeated. France's efforts to control Vietnam were seen as part of the containment policy to protect the free world from communist expansion, not colonialism.

The consensus on American containment policy was made clear when Dwight D. Eisenhower became president in January 1953. He agreed with the logic and assumptions of Truman's policy and continued his efforts to support the French in Vietnam. Indeed, according to Eisenhower's secretary of state, John Foster Dulles, the administration saw the situation in Vietnam as "even more dangerous in its global aspects than is the fighting in Korea, for a collapse in Indo-China would have immediate grave reactions in other areas of Asia."[27] When Eisenhower set out the bipolar worldview that containment was based on in his inaugural address on January 20, 1953, that "freedom is pitted against slavery; lightness against the dark," Vietnam was one of the places he had in mind. The struggle there conferred "a common dignity upon the French soldier who dies in Indo-China . . . [and] the American life given in Korea."[28] The president called upon the nation to do more in East Asia, and asked Congress "to make substantial additional resources available to assist the French and the Associated States in their military efforts to defeat Communist Viet Minh aggression."[29]

Eisenhower summarized the importance he placed on Indochina to the "free world" at his famous press conference on April 7, 1954, where he outlined the "domino theory":

> First of all, you have the specific value of a locality in its production of materials that the world needs. Then you have the possibility that many human beings pass under a dictatorship that is inimical to the free world. Finally, you have broader considerations that might follow what you would call the "falling domino" principle. You have a row of dominoes set up, you knock over the first one, and what will happen to the last one is the certainty that it will go over very quickly. So you could have the beginning of a disintegration that would have the most profound influences.

Eisenhower noted that for the first point, tin, tungsten, rubber, and other items would be lost. More importantly, the free world could not afford greater losses in Asia where "already some 450 million of its people" have fallen "to the Communist dictatorship." Finally, the loss of Indochina to communism would lead to the loss "of Burma, of Thailand, of the Peninsula, and Indonesia" and threats against Japan, Taiwan, the Philippines, and eventually Australia and New Zealand. In addition, it would deny Japan that region where it must trade or "Japan, in turn, will have only one place in the world to go—that is, toward the Communist areas in order to live. So, the possible consequences of the loss are just incalculable to the free world."[30]

It was not, however, possible to just grant independence to Vietnam. As Dulles lamented in January 1954, the "principal difficulty in the way now of achieving independence there is the lack of political maturity on the part of the people themselves, and their inability to make up their own minds as to what it is they want." The secretary of state continued by noting that he was "a great believer in the general idea of giving independence to people who want it, but I think that—I don't know really whether some of these people are qualified, well qualified yet for independence. I am not sure that these people are qualified to be fully independent." The communists tested the Filipinos' capacity for independence, but they had years of American tutelage and "quite a lot of experience and training and development." Granting "independence to a lot of these people in a world where the Communists are prowling around to grab you, it is not a thing which is easily accomplished." The great question mark to be overcome remained whom one would work with and "whether there is a political maturity among the people to organize their own institutions, establish a strong government needed to meet the disturbing conditions that prevail there."[31]

Dulles explained to the Senate Foreign Relations Committee (SFRC) that "the trouble comes when you come practically to translating that change of attitude into the life of the community. What you have got there is a bunch of people who have been colonialists all their lives, and it is in the actual working relations, who has what house, do you bring them into your clubs, and do you allow them to be trained in units larger than a battalion . . . are what really makes the difference." Change would not come easily due to the lack of abilities among the Vietnamese and because "we all know how difficult it is to change social relations which have grown up over a long period of years, which reflect the white man's sense of superiority, the ruler's sense of superiority over the natives."[32] This meant that Vietnam needed some Western nation to protect it or it would fall to the international communist movement.

With France's defeat at Dienbienphu in May 1954, the crisis had to be turned into an opportunity. With the

French failure, it was now best to remove them altogether and start anew with an American-selected leader and American advisors. Dulles emphasized that the fundamental question was that of independence. This was "a war for independence, not a war for colonialism." From that perspective, the United States could now intervene directly. There should be, he told Congress, "a more effective participation by the United States in the training of native forces," building on past successes in Greece, the Philippines, and Korea where the "United States has done an excellent job of training other people." The United States could clearly succeed where France had failed. "I think we have shown a certain aptitude," Dulles declared, "and developed a type of officer who can do that sort of thing." There was plenty of local manpower; it just needed the proper direction and training that only the United States could provide.[33] Dulles was ready to embark upon the task of building a new nation to block communist control of all of Southeast Asia and to provide a showcase for American-supported independence that would be a middle ground, a third way created by the United States, between colonialism and communism that would allow true nationalism, that is, pro-Western, to develop in Vietnam.

The Geneva Accords that brought an end to the fighting between the French and the Vietminh provided for an armistice and a temporary military partition of Vietnam at the 17th parallel with the Vietminh pulling its forces to the north and the French to the south. These were to be administrative units designed to separate the two armies. Neither side was to allow foreign military bases or enter into military alliances. The political question was to be resolved by elections, supervised by an international commission, to be held within two years to establish a unified Vietnam.

Dulles immediately made it clear that the United States was not bound by the settlements reached at Geneva and that the Eisenhower administration's intention was to work against the enactment of the provisions. In particular, he noted that in Vietnam, unlike Germany or Korea, the United States "was not anxious to see an early election" held "because as things stand today, it is probable that Ho Chi Minh would get a very large vote."[34] Eisenhower wrote in his memoirs that "I have never talked or corresponded with a person knowledgeable in Indochinese affairs who did not agree that had elections been held as of the time of the fighting, possibly 80 per cent of the population would have voted for the Communist Ho Chi Minh as their leader rather than Chief of State Bao Dai." He continued by noting that the lack of leadership demonstrated by Bao Dai had led the Vietnamese to believe they had nothing to fight for.[35]

Ideally, Dulles would favor "genuinely free elections" in Vietnam, but currently it was not possible. "At the present time in a country which is politically immature, which has been the scene of civil war and disruption, we would doubt whether the immediate conditions would be conducive to a result which would really reflect the will of the people." Further, the United States would not "stand passively by and see the extension of communism by any means into Southeast Asia."[36] Dulles did not believe that the people of Southeast Asia could govern themselves. Without continued guidance from the West, these nations would fall to communism. American officials believed that until the Vietnamese gained the same level of political maturity that American guidance had provided the Filipinos, they would need support, and that the United States was obligated, in the face of France's failure, to provide it. What was necessary was a strong anticommunist leader who could combat

Ho's forces and develop South Vietnam with the backing of the United States. That would allow time for the people to learn the benefits of a U.S.-supported government as opposed to the current conditions. At that point, they could cast ballots that were more informed.

Success in South Vietnam would take two years, Dulles believed, "and would require in large part taking over the training responsibility by the US."[37] Still, it could be done. As Dulles told a friend, with the French defeat "we have a clean base there now without a taint of colonialism. Dienbienphu was a blessing in disguise."[38] Over and over, administration officials pointed to the examples of Greece, Iran, and most notably the Philippines as proof that they could build a new nation in South Vietnam. American policy makers saw the progress of the Philippines from chaos to order and the defeat of communism as a remarkable success story they could take full credit for, a shining example of American leadership and nation building. The United States had backed Ramon Magsaysay first for the position of secretary of defense and in 1953 for president at a time when the communist-led Huk rebellion threatened to overthrow the government in Manila. He was credited with suppressing the Huk uprising and averting economic collapse in the archipelago. This was mainly due, officials believed, to his willingness to listen to and follow American advice. Magsaysay had secured a strategic outpost of the United States, established order, and turned the newly independent former colony firmly toward the west.[39] If the United States could successfully create a stable, independent, pro-U.S. Philippines, it could do the same in South Vietnam.

The man the United States entrusted to effect its political will in Vietnam was Ngo Dinh Diem. Bao Dai appointed him premier of South Vietnam on June 17, 1954. Diem, a Catholic, enjoyed important political support within the United States, particularly from leading Catholic politicians such as Senators Mike Mansfield and John F. Kennedy, and the American Friends of Vietnam, a nonpartisan lobby. In August, the United States informed France that it intended to deal directly with the new state of South Vietnam and that it would no longer funnel aid through Paris or have its military advisors work with French officers. The Eisenhower administration's decision was motivated by Cold War concerns. It was essential, Dulles argued, that "in South Vietnam a strong Nationalist Government . . . be developed and supported if the world is not to witness an early Communist take-over in Indochina and a still greater menace to South and Southeast Asia with repercussions in Africa." In order to help ensure its success and "preserve freedom in Vietnam," the United States would now treat Diem's government as an independent state and American assistance would be sent directly to it "rather than through the French government."[40]

It all seemed to rest on Diem's ability, with the assistance of Colonel Edward Geary Lansdale, to rule with a strong hand. Dulles personally selected Lansdale to assist Diem because he was seen as an expert in nation building. He had been the closest American advisor to Magsaysay in the Philippines and was brought over to Saigon to repeat that performance. There were many questions to be answered. Could Diem become a strong leader? Was it possible to build around Diem "a government which with our . . . support will be relatively enduring and may eventually attract the allegiance of the three sects and the Army?"[41] With Lansdale on the scene, and American advisors, money, and know-how, the administration believed the answer to these questions was yes.

Diem's stock rose in the spring of 1955 when his army was able to defeat the powerful sects with their private armies in Saigon and establish his government as the only noncommunist force in the nation. The administration was now fully committed to Diem and was determined not to fail. With American support secure, Diem informed Ho's government in Hanoi that he would not participate in the elections stipulated by the Geneva Accords. The State Department encouraged Diem in his position. An intelligence analysis in 1955 found that "almost any type of election would . . . give the Communists a very significant if not a decisive advantage." Instead, Diem held a referendum to form a republic with himself as the president. The choice was his new Republic of Vietnam or the continuation of the State of Vietnam under Bao Dai. In an election that he fully controlled, Diem garnered over 98% of the vote.[42]

For his efforts, Diem received unvarnished praise in the United States. Apparently a Magsaysay had been found for Vietnam. Dulles reported to the Senate that American faith in Diem had been rewarded. The "situation has immensely improved. . . . We stuck with Diem at a time when many people, including some in our own Government, felt he should be abandoned." Diem, he continued, "has done a wonderful job, of course with our help, in cleaning up his sect armies," and "Diem's authority throughout the area is now generally accepted." The problems were not all yet solved, but Diem had "brought central authority into the country to a degree which is really quite amazing." Furthermore, "Bao Dai has been eliminated, and there is a chance for really building a strong and effective anti-Communist regime in an area where for a time it looked as though it would be swept away as a result of the French defeat . . . and by the unfavorable armistice terms."[43]

Senator Kennedy praised Diem for making South Vietnam "the cornerstone of the Free World in Southeast Asia, the keystone in the arch, the finger in the dike," while Mansfield argued that the fact "that a free Viet Nam exists at the present time . . . is the result of the efforts of Mr. Diem."[44] The *Saturday Evening Post* referred to Diem as the "mandarin in a sharkskin suit who's upsetting the Red timetable."[45] The *New York Times* entitled its 1957 profile on Diem "An Asian Liberator." It applauded his work to "save his country from falling apart" and how he "tirelessly toured the countryside so that the people would get to know him and perhaps like him more than they did Ho Chi Minh." This effort was paying off as the "Vietnamese learn to respect their new Government and their new leader."[46]

American officials believed that the United States could do what France could not, create a pro-Western nationalism in Vietnam and build a nation that would provide a stable anticommunist government and a third way for other nations in Asia and Africa to follow as they gained independence. The temporary successes Diem enjoyed lulled Washington into a false sense of security that American policy was correct and succeeding, and served to mask the fundamental flaws in American policy. Policy makers viewed and understood Vietnam primarily as a part of the Cold War and not as a real and distinct place with a history and people who were acting on their own local needs and desires. The hubris of Washington that with the right effort an American story would develop in South Vietnam allowed officials to ignore the ongoing revolution in Vietnam and talk instead of containment, nation building, and falling dominoes.

ESCALATION

During the 1960 presidential campaign, Kennedy charged that the Eisenhower administration had allowed a missile gap to develop that placed the United States dangerously behind the Soviet Union in weaponry and technology. Moreover, Eisenhower had allowed communism into the Western Hemisphere with the fall of Cuba to Fidel Castro, a sign that the United States was also losing the battle for the allegiance of the Third World. More Cubas could be expected unless dramatic action was taken. While some of this rhetoric was a political turning of the tables on the Republicans for their claims in the 1952 campaign that the Democrats had lost China, it also reflected the political realities of the Cold War that Americans expected their leaders to prevent the spread of communism, and belief in the universality of American values, institutions, and policies and the ability of the United States to control political change in the world.

In his inaugural address, Kennedy set forth his promise that he would regain the initiative in the Cold War struggles with the Soviet Union and defend America's global interests. He declared that the United States "shall pay any price, bear any burden, meet any hardship, support any friend, oppose any foe to assure the survival and the success of liberty." The young president embodied American optimism and confidence, boldly stating that "In the long history of the world, only a few generations have been granted the role of defending freedom in its hour of maximum danger. I do not shrink from this responsibility—I welcome it." He believed, as did his fellow citizens, that the "energy, the faith, the devotion which we bring to this endeavor will light our country and all who serve it—and the glow from that fire can truly light the world."[47]

Yet when Kennedy took office, the American effort at creating a viable, independent, and noncommunist South Vietnam was in trouble. The formation of the National Liberation Front (NLF) in 1960 and the resumption of fighting exposed all of the weaknesses of the Diem regime and its lack of widespread support among the peasants of South Vietnam. Despite American military and economic aid, Diem alienated most of the population while the Army of the Republic of Vietnam (ARVN) was proving unable and/or unwilling to effectively combat NLF guerrillas. The Kennedy administration had to find some method to overcome the fact that the Saigon government was an unpopular American creation, rather than a solid Vietnamese structure. It would demand an escalation of the American commitment to ensure that South Vietnam did not fall to communism.

Moreover, in the wake of the debacle at the Bay of Pigs, where American-backed anticommunist Cubans failed in an attempt to oust Castro from power, Kennedy needed to prove his determination to fight the Cold War and the credibility of American commitments overseas. Speaking to the American Society of Newspaper Editors on April 20, 1961, Kennedy made the connection between events in Cuba and Vietnam and his commitment to action clear. "We dare not fail to see the insidious nature of this new and deeper struggle," he warned the nation. "We dare not fail to grasp the new concepts, the new tools, the new sense of urgency we will need to combat it—whether in Cuba or South Vietnam." The message was the same. "The complacent, the self-indulgent, the soft societies are about to be swept away with the debris of history. Only the strong, only the industrious, only the determined, only the courageous, only the visionary who determine the real nature of our struggle can possibly survive." Kennedy was prepared for the challenge and to use any methods necessary for victory.[48] As the president told the reporter James Reston, if Khrushchev believed that he had "no guts . . . we won't get anywhere with him. So we have to act." That meant taking the initiative in Vietnam. "We have a problem in trying to make our power credible," Kennedy stated, "and Vietnam looks like the place."[49]

The American commitment to Vietnam had to be deepened because the struggle was too central to American national interests to leave to the Vietnamese. To demonstrate his commitment, Kennedy sent Vice President Lyndon Johnson to Vietnam to meet with Diem and to assure him of American support. Johnson's report to Kennedy left little room for doubt as to the importance he placed on Vietnam. "The battle against Communism must be joined in Southeast Asia with strength and determination to achieve success there," Johnson wrote, "or the United States, inevitably, must surrender the Pacific and take up our defenses on our own shores." At this point, American forces were not required. The United States did, however, need to increase its aid programs, and the number of military advisors and civilian technicians, to allow Saigon to win the war. What Vietnam required, Johnson stressed, was "the attention of our very best talents—under the very closest Washington direction—on matters economic, military and political." The vice president declared that "the basic decision in Southeast Asia is here. We must decide whether to help these countries to the best of our ability or throw in the towel in the area and pull back our defenses to San Francisco and a 'Fortress America' concept." The government in Saigon was not, for Johnson, the key to the situation. That rested in Washington, DC, and the willingness of the administration to act. "The country can be saved—if we move quickly and wisely," Johnson reported. "We must have coordination of purpose in our country team, diplomatic and military. The most important thing is imaginative, creative, American management of our military aid program."[50]

Following the advice of Johnson and his other top advisors, Kennedy dramatically escalated the U.S. effort and presence in Vietnam. From 1961 to 1963 the president increased the number of American military advisors from 500 to over 16,000, initiated the Strategic Hamlet program designed to protect villagers from NLF intimidation, provided more sophisticated military equipment to the ARVN, and placed a greater emphasis on counterinsurgency measures and training by the Green Berets. None of these efforts proved sufficient to turn the tide of the military battle or increase the effectiveness or popularity of the Diem regime. Indeed, by the summer of 1963, many American officials were deciding that if the war and the preservation of South Vietnam were left in the hands of Diem, the United States would suffer a tremendous defeat.

The year 1963 began with the stunning defeat of ARVN forces in the battle of Ap Bac where the South Vietnamese military held all the advantages but still managed to snatch defeat from the jaws of victory. An NLF battalion that was surrounded by a superior number of ARVN troops supported by tanks, artillery, and air power managed to escape due to the unwillingness of South Vietnamese commanders to fully engage the battle.[51] By the summer, discontent with the rule of Diem exploded into protests by noncommunist students and Buddhists. The most dramatic of these demonstrations were a series of self-immolations by Buddhist monks. Diem, and his brother Ngo Dinh Nhu, who headed the secret police, responded with attacks against their political enemies, massive arrests, and the closing of

Buddhist pagodas. Nhu's wife likened the self-immolations to barbecues and stated she would welcome more. Diem stubbornly refused to criticize her actions or distance himself from his brother and his brutal tactics.

There were few alternatives to Diem. Outside of the military, all other noncommunist groups were willing to negotiate a settlement with the NLF to end the war, a position that the United States rejected. Having supported Diem and his repressive government for almost a decade, Washington found that there was no political center and that it held far less leverage with Diem than it thought. That left only the military to impose order, hold the society together, and prosecute the war. After numerous efforts failed to convince Diem to change his course, broaden the composition of his government, and fire his brother, the Kennedy administration signaled the South Vietnamese generals that it would support a coup. The fault, according to administration officials, lay completely with Diem and not American policy. Ambassador Lodge informed Washington that the Diem government was "essentially a medieval, Oriental despotism of the classic family type" that understood "few, if any, of the arts of popular government."[52] A coup was necessary to complete the U.S. effort of bringing "this medieval country into the 20th century." Considerable progress had been made in "military and economic ways but to gain victory we must also bring them into the 20th century politically and that can only be done by either a thoroughgoing change in the behavior of the present government or by another government."[53]

The talk of a coup in early September, however, fizzled as the generals squabbled among themselves and worried about betrayal to Nhu's secret police. The United States, Kennedy stated, still had to "find an effective means of changing the political atmosphere in Saigon" in order to improve the long-term military outlook. This was because of the "harm which Diem's political actions are causing to the effort against the Viet Cong rather than on our moral opposition to the kind of government Diem is running."[54] (Viet Cong and VC were American shorthand for Vietnamese Communists or the NLF.) With assurances of support from Washington, plotting for a coup resumed in Saigon. On November 1, 1963, the South Vietnamese military moved against the Diem government. Diem and Nhu surrendered in exchange for safe passage out of the country. Once arrested, however, both were killed. Three weeks later, Kennedy was assassinated in Dallas and the problems of Vietnam fell onto the shoulders of Lyndon B. Johnson.

The new president would continue the elusive pursuit of the right leader to rescue the American effort in Vietnam. Comments concerning reform and winning the hearts and minds of the South Vietnamese notwithstanding, the main purpose of the government in Saigon was to fight the war against the NLF and North Vietnam. As Johnson stated upon becoming president, "I am not going to lose Vietnam. I am not going to be the President who saw Southeast Asia go the way China went."[55] There was no questioning of the basic assumptions of American policy by the Johnson administration, just a quest for better leadership. It was now the South Vietnamese military's job to do what Diem could not: stabilize the political situation in Saigon and win the war.

This, however, did not happen. During Johnson's first fourteen months as president, there were over a half-dozen changes in the government of South Vietnam. Each time, Johnson assured the new military leaders of American support and steadily increased the level of aid and American military advisors to Saigon. To strengthen his hand and demonstrate American resolve, Johnson took advantage of unreliable reports of an attack on American naval vessels in early August 1964 to secure passage of the Gulf of Tonkin Resolution, which authorized the president to use whatever force he deemed necessary to protect American interests in Vietnam. Demonstrating the bipartisan nature of the support for containment, it passed the House of Representatives by a vote of 416-0 and the Senate 88-2. As he moved to pass the landmark Civil Rights Act of 1964, implement his War on Poverty, and launch his Great Society programs, Johnson could not afford to be attacked as soft on communism in an election year. The Gulf of Tonkin Resolution demonstrated he would stand up to communist aggression. Nonetheless, Johnson moved cautiously, not wanting to make Vietnam a major issue and hoping that the ARVN, with American support, could find a way to defeat the NLF and maintain a noncommunist South Vietnam.

The political chaos was matched by a military decline as well. National Security Advisor McGeorge Bundy wrote the president on January 27, 1965, that he and Secretary of Defense Robert McNamara were "now pretty well convinced that our current policy can lead only to disastrous defeat." The policy of providing massive aid, military assistance, and advice while waiting "for a stable government" had proven to be a failure. "There is no real hope of success in this area unless and until our own policy and priorities change."[56] Now, confronted by the possibility of South Vietnam falling to communism, Johnson was facing the decision of whether to take over the war from the Vietnamese in order to ensure the continuation of the American-backed regime in Saigon.

Bundy argued that the "underlying difficulties in Saigon arise from the spreading conviction there that the future is without hope for anti-Communists." America's friends were discouraged by a lack of action on Washington's part in the face of the known advances being made by the NLF in the countryside. Bundy and McNamara concluded that the United States had to abandon its "essentially passive role which can only lead to eventual defeat and an invitation to get out in humiliating circumstances." Two alternative policies were outlined for Johnson. The first, which Bundy and McNamara favored, was the use of American "military power . . . to force a change of Communist policy." The second was to seek a negotiated settlement to salvage what could be preserved with no additional military risks. This amounted to defeat under a different guise.[57] Johnson's response was unequivocal. "Stable government or no stable government, we'll do what we have to do—we will move strongly. I'm prepared to do that."[58]

The first step was the authorization of Operation Rolling Thunder, a sustained bombing campaign against North Vietnam. Begun in February 1965, Rolling Thunder was designed to demonstrate the power of the United States and its commitment to the defense of South Vietnam. In theory, this action would destroy both the North's capacity and will to resist while demonstrating to Hanoi that the costs of continued fighting outweighed any potential gain. At that point, North Vietnam would abandon the NLF and negotiate a settlement on American terms. The bombing had another purpose as well, to strengthen the government in Saigon by proving the willingness of the United States to fight for its survival. Most senior officials, however, never believed that the bombing campaign was the final answer to the problems of maintaining a noncommunist government in South Vietnam. It did, however, buy the administration time while it debated the decision to send American troops to Vietnam.[59]

Facing a situation where a continuation of the status quo meant defeat, Johnson inched ever closer to escalating the war by sending in American troops. In March, the first marine units landed in Danang to protect American air bases. More followed in April, and the first Army units arrived in May. On April 7, 1965, Johnson spoke at Johns Hopkins University where he explained to the nation why he believed the United States had to escalate its commitment to South Vietnam and fight.

His speech drew upon all of the verities of the Cold War and containment. The war in Vietnam was cast as the central confrontation in the Cold War with the forces of international communism. It was, therefore, presented as vital to American security and prosperity. "We fight," Johnson declared, "because we must fight if we are to live in a world where every country can shape its own destiny, and only in such a world will our own freedom be finally secure." The president presented the conflict as a clear case of communist aggression and expansion, and not a civil war or revolutionary struggle within Vietnam. "The first reality," Johnson explained, "is that North Viet-nam has attacked the independent nation of South Viet-nam. Its object is total conquest." North Vietnam, however, was just a puppet of the communist superpowers and the war a piece of a larger communist effort to conquer all of Asia. Johnson warned his audience that "over this war—and all Asia—is another reality: the deepening shadow of Communist China. The rulers of Hanoi are urged on by Peking. . . . It is a nation which is helping the forces of violence in almost every continent. The contest in Viet-nam is part of a wider pattern of aggressive purposes."[60]

The president insisted that it was essential that the United States meet this challenge, demonstrate its credibility and willingness to uphold its containment doctrine, and avoid another Munich. Johnson reminded his audience that his policy was a continuation of the Truman Doctrine, and that "since 1954 every American President has offered support to the people of South Viet-nam. We have helped to build, and we have helped to defend. . . . To dishonor that pledge, to abandon this small and brave nation to its enemies . . . would be an unforgivable wrong." The damage, Johnson believed, would go well beyond Vietnam to the confidence of America's allies in its word and support, and American credibility. American action in Vietnam would strengthen world order because "around the globe from Berlin to Thailand are people whose well being rests in part on the belief that they can count on us if they are attacked. To leave Viet-nam to its fate would shake the confidence of all these people in the value of an American commitment and in the value of America's word. The result would be increased unrest and instability, and even wider war." The lesson of Munich, to Johnson, was clear and applied to Vietnam. "Let no one think for a moment that retreat from Viet-nam would bring an end to conflict. The battle would be renewed in one country and then another. The central lesson of our time is that the appetite of aggression is never satisfied. To withdraw from one battlefield means only to prepare for the next."[61]

Lyndon Johnson was convinced that the application of American force would crush the opposition and be a decisive moment in the Cold War. As he noted, the American military buildup was being undertaken "to convince the leaders of North Viet-nam—and all who seek to share their conquest—of a simple fact: We will not be defeated. We will not grow tired. We will not withdraw, either openly or under the cloak of a meaningless agreement."[62] In his policy and optimism, Johnson reflected the beliefs of the nation.

Containment enjoyed bipartisan support and it had to be upheld. American credibility was on the line. Recent history demanded action to stem the tide of communist aggression. At the same time, it appeared to demonstrate that whenever the United States committed itself to a cause it succeeded.

On June 26, 1965, McNamara informed the president that "the VC are winning" the war. There were three options: cut U.S. losses and withdraw, continue the current policy with the hope that the situation would improve "while recognizing that our position will probably grow weaker, or escalating the American military commitment to defeat the NLF and force negotiations on U.S. terms." The secretary of defense recommended to Johnson the third choice. The other two spelled an unacceptable defeat.[63] At the meeting of senior administration officials to discuss McNamara's proposal, only Undersecretary of State George Ball dissented, arguing that the United States could not win a guerrilla war in Southeast Asia. Everyone else agreed that it was essential for the United States to send its own troops to uphold containment, and the burden of proof was on Ball to demonstrate otherwise. Johnson told Ball that if he followed his advice, "wouldn't all those countries say Uncle Sam is a paper tiger—wouldn't we lose credibility breaking the word of three presidents. . . . It would seem to be an irreparable blow." Bundy concurred, noting that "the world, the country, and the [Vietnamese] would have alarming reactions if we got out," while Secretary of State Dean Rusk declared that "if the Communist world finds out we will not pursue our commitment to the end, I don't know where they will stay their hand." Ambassador Lodge made the link to Munich explicit, arguing that a failure to act would be appeasement, and that "there is a greater threat to World War III if we don't go in."[64]

All the logic and rationale of the Cold War and containment called for escalation, and Johnson agreed to increase American troop strength to 125,000 immediately and 200,000 by the end of the year, with more forces to be sent as needed. French and South Vietnamese forces may have failed, but American leaders were certain that the United States, the world's richest and most powerful nation, could force its will on a poor, peasant nation. The "loss" of South Vietnam was politically unthinkable and presumably unnecessary given American might.

The United States, therefore, would fight a limited war in Vietnam to uphold the policy of containment, deter aggression, and demonstrate American credibility and resolve without engaging in a direct conflict with the communist superpowers, the USSR and China, that could escalate into a global conflict. The policy was designed to meet communist aggression early, preventing another Munich and a general war, without having to sacrifice the Great Society or demanding sacrifices from the American people. Vietnam was important due to the Cold War and how it fit within this global policy of confrontation with what American leaders termed monolithic, international communism. The strategy to be employed was a war of attrition that would take advantage of American firepower and technological superiority to increase the costs of the war on the enemy to a point that they could no longer sustain the fighting or found the losses they were suffering greater than any gain they could hope for. At this point, they would yield, and the United States would have succeeded in containing communism and preserving South Vietnam.

When President Johnson announced on July 28, 1965, an open-ended escalation of American forces in Vietnam, he had the nation's support. Typical were the comments in *Life* and *Time* magazines that reflected the consensus in American society on foreign policy. Employing the Munich analogy, *Life* opined that "it was wiser and takes less bloodshed to stop a bid for world tyranny early rather than late." The editors went on to endorse Johnson's policy as necessary for the security of the nation, noting that "it is also wise as well as moral to fulfill a promise to defend a victim of attack. . . . In this sense our Vietnam policy is a moral policy, and most Americans fortunately see it that way." *Time* called the Vietnam War "The Right War at the Right Time," because it was a "crucial test of American policy and will" by the communist world.[65] The sending of American troops to Vietnam was justified by the policy of containment. Communism was aggressive, expansive, and monolithic. South Vietnam was being attacked by North Vietnam, which was acting in the interests of China and the Soviet Union. Twenty years of the Cold War consensus on the necessity of containing communism had led Americans to believe that the events in Vietnam were a threat to their security and prosperity.

Moreover, success seemed assured. It was a limited war, one American forces could and would win in a short period of time. On what basis was there reason to think otherwise? As Philip Caputo, one of the first Marines to land at Danang in March 1965, recalled, "for Americans who did not come of age in the early sixties, it may be hard to grasp what those years were like—the pride and overpowering self-assurance that prevailed." To the postwar generation, "America seemed omnipotent then: the country could still claim it had never lost a war, and we believed we were ordained to play cop to the Communists' robber and spread our own political faith around the world." Vietnam was the front line of the Cold War and the place to protect the American Century. "We saw ourselves," Caputo continued, "as the champions of 'a cause that was destined to triumph.' So, when we marched into the rice paddies . . . we carried, along with our packs and rifles, the implicit convictions that the Viet Cong would be quickly beaten and that we were doing something altogether noble and good."[66] It was this optimism, confidence, indeed hubris, and one's ability to continue to believe in the idea of an American Century, the verities of the Cold War, and the correctness of America's actions, that were central to the debates over the Tet Offensive and among its most important casualties.

NOTES

1. Henry Luce, "The American Century," in William Appleman Williams et al., *America in Vietnam: A Documentary History* (Garden City: Doubleday, 1985), 22–27.

2. Luce, "The American Century," 22–27.

3. *Public Papers of the Presidents: Harry S. Truman, 1947* (Washington, DC: Government Printing Office, 1963), 167–70.

4. Quoted in Melvyn P. Leffler, *The Specter of Communism: The United States and the Origins of the Cold War, 1917–1953* (New York: Hill and Wang, 1994), 52.

5. Department of State, *Foreign Relations of the United States: 1946* (Washington, DC: Government Printing Office), VI:699–701 (hereafter *FRUS* followed by year and volume).

6. *FRUS: 1946*, VII:840–42.

7. Alonzo Hamby, *Man of the People: A Life of Harry S. Truman* (New York: Oxford University Press, 1995), 353–54.

8. For a summary of these concerns, see NSC, "Review of the World Situation as It Relates to the Security of the United States," September 12, 1947, Records of the National Security Council, Box 1, HSTL.

9. Dean Acheson, *Present at the Creation: My Years in the State Department* (New York, Norton, 1969), 219.

10. *Public Papers of the Presidents: Truman, 1947*, 176–80.

11. Roosevelt to Hull, January 24, 1944, in Williams et al., *America in Vietnam*, 30.

12. See Lloyd Gardner, *Approaching Vietnam: From World War II through Dienbienphu, 1941–1954* (New York: Norton, 1988), 21–53.

13. Samuel Rosenman, ed., *Public Papers and Addresses of Franklin D. Roosevelt, 1944–45* (New York: Random House, 1950), 556–65.

14. *FRUS: 1945*, I:121–24.

15. *FRUS: 1945*, VI:307.

16. Memorandum for the President, Division of Far East Affairs, April 21, 1945, "American Policy with Respect to Indochina," in Gareth Porter, ed., *Vietnam: A History in Documents* (New York: New American Library, 1979), 22.

17. Archimedes Patti, *Why Viet Nam?: Prelude to America's Albatross* (Berkeley: University of California Press, 1980), 382.

18. *FRUS: 1947*, VI:95–97.

19. Quoted in Williams et al., *America in Vietnam*, 95.

20. Quoted in Williams et al., *America in Vietnam*, 90–92.

21. *FRUS: 1949*, VII:29–30.

22. *FRUS: 1950*, VI:711–15.

23. *Public Papers of the Presidents: Truman, 1951* (Washington, DC: Government Printing Office, 1965), 223–27.

24. *Public Papers of the Presidents: Truman, 1951*, 223–27.

25. Quoted in Patti, *Why Viet Nam?*, 389.

26. *FRUS: 1950*, VI:878–79.

27. United States, Congress: Senate, *Executive Sessions of the Senate Foreign Relations Committee, 1953* (Washington, DC: Government Printing Office), V:139–40 (hereafter *Executive Sessions* followed by the year and volume).

28. *Public Papers of the Presidents: Dwight D. Eisenhower, 1953* (Washington, DC: Government Printing Office, 1960), 4.

29. *Public Papers of the Presidents: Eisenhower, 1953*, 258.

30. *Public Papers of the Presidents: Eisenhower, 1954* (Washington, DC: Government Printing Office, 1960), 382–83.

31. *Executive Sessions*, 1954, VI:23–24.

32. *Executive Sessions*, 1953, V:386–88.

33. *Executive Sessions*, 1954, VI:267–77.

34. *Executive Sessions*, 1954, VI:642–43.

35. Dwight D. Eisenhower, *Mandate For Change, 1953–1956* (Garden City: Doubleday, 1963), 372.

36. Quoted in Gardner, *Approaching Vietnam*, 270.

37. Quoted in Gardner, *Approaching Vietnam*, 258.

38. Quoted in Marilyn Young, *The Vietnam Wars, 1945–1990* (New York: HarperCollins, 1991), 46.

39. Stanley Karnow, *In Our Image: America's Empire in the Philippines* (New York: Random House, 1989), 346–55.

40. Dulles to Eisenhower, August 18, 1954; Dulles to Mendes-France, August 16, 1954, AWF, DH Series, Box 4, DDEL.

41. *FRUS: 1952-54*, XIII (Part 2):2085–86.

42. Young, *Vietnam Wars*, 52–53.

43. *Executive Sessions*, 1956, VIII:160; see also 249th Meeting of the NSC, May 19, 1955, AWF, NSC Series, DDEL.

44. Quoted in Lauren Baritz, *Backfire: A History of How American Culture Led Us into Vietnam and Made Us Fight the Way We Did* (New York: Morrow, 1985), 96; Gregory Allen Olson, *Mansfield and Vietnam: A Study in Rhetorical Adaptations* (East Lansing: Michigan State University Press, 1995), 74.

45. Quoted in Frances Fitzgerald, *Fire in the Lake* (Boston: Little, Brown, 1972), 114.

46. Quoted in Young, *The Vietnam Wars*, 58.

47. *Public Papers of the Presidents: John F. Kennedy, 1961* (Washington, DC: Government Printing Office, 1962), 1–3.

48. *Public Papers of the Presidents: Kennedy, 1961*, 304–06.

49. Quoted in Lloyd Gardner, *Pay Any Price: Lyndon Johnson and the Wars for Vietnam* (Chicago: Ivan Dee, 1995), 47.

50. Johnson to Kennedy, May 23, 1961, NSF: Bundy Files, Boxes 18 and 19, LBJL.

51. Neil Sheehan, *A Bright Shining Lie: John Paul Vann and America in Vietnam* (New York: Random House, 1988), 203–65.

52. Quoted in Gardner, *Pay Any Price*, 81.

THE AMERICAN ROAD TO VIETNAM

53. Quoted in Gardner, *Pay Any Price*, 85.

54. Summary Record of National Security Council Meeting, October 2, 1963, NSF: Box 314, JFKL.

55. Quoted in Gardner, *Pay Any Price*, 87.

56. Bundy to Johnson, "Basic Policy in Vietnam," January 27, 1965, NSF: Memos to the President, Bundy, Box 2, LBJL.

57. Bundy to Johnson, "Basic Policy in Vietnam," January 27, 1965, NSF: Memos to the President, Bundy, Box 2, LBJL.

58. Gardner, *Pay Any Price*, 167.

59. Young, *The Vietnam Wars*, 135–42.

60. *Public Papers of the Presidents: Lyndon B. Johnson, 1965* (Washington, DC: Government Printing Office, 1966), I:394–98.

61. *Public Papers of the Presidents: Lyndon B. Johnson, 1965*, 394–98.

62. *Public Papers of the Presidents: Lyndon B. Johnson, 1965*, 394–98.

63. *FRUS: 1964–68*, III: 97–104.

64. Minutes of Meeting, July 21, 1965, President, 1963–1969, Meeting Notes File, Box I, LBJL.

65. Quoted in Terry Anderson, *The Movement and the Sixties* (New York: Oxford University Press, 1995), 136–37.

66. Philip Caputo, *A Rumor of War* (New York: Ballantine Books, 1977), xiii–xvi.

Chapter Two

LIGHT AT THE END OF THE TUNNEL

THE WAR IN VIETNAM WAS, FOR AMERICAN LEADERS, a test of wills between the United States and its enemies. A war of attrition rather than one of conquest. The United States did not seek to destroy or capture North Vietnam, but to preserve the anticommunist government in Saigon, uphold containment, and demonstrate American credibility to its allies and adversaries. To accomplish these goals, the United States escalated both the air and ground wars to crush the enemy's capacity and will for fighting. The operating assumption behind American strategy was straightforward. As the United States raised the costs of the war, the North Vietnamese and National Liberation Front (NLF) would realize that Ho Chi Minh's policy of aggression, as Washington understood it, could not succeed, and that the costs outweighed any gains. Hence, the United States had to inflict as much damage as possible to demonstrate to its enemy that their cause was hopeless.

To Washington's surprise, the NLF and the North Vietnamese did not crumble under the weight of American firepower and met United States escalation with their own. American policy makers expected the Vietnamese to understand the war on the same terms Washington did, as a limited war to block the expansion of monolithic communism and maintain the anticommunist Saigon government in the South. Many Vietnamese, however, believed that the NLF and Ho Chi Minh represented Vietnamese nationalism and independence. Thus, they were willing to endure enormous casualties, suffering, and destruction to continue to inflict losses on American forces and avoid defeat. Hanoi and the NLF understood that American military strength made it impossible for them to achieve a victory on the battlefield. Their strategy of protracted war was to demonstrate Saigon's lack of legitimacy and inability to rule, and to win their own war of attrition against the will of the United States to fight a long, drawn-out, and inconclusive war.

The continued escalation of troops and costs with no apparent progress, along with the growing questions concerning the rationale for the war, led to a public debate in the United States over the nature and wisdom of the fighting that eroded support for the war. By 1967, it appeared to many that the best the American forces could attain was a bloody and frustrating stalemate. This belief led to public criticisms of the war and calls for negotiations and withdrawal. American officials in both Washington and Saigon rejected this view. They countered their critics by reaffirming the logic of containment and the necessity of the war for American security and credibility and presenting an optimistic account of progress and claims at the end of 1967 that the United States was winning the conflict. The administration claimed there was light at the end of the tunnel.

ESCALATION AND DISSENT

Operation Rolling Thunder was steadily increased over the next three years, from 63,000 tons of bombs in 1965 to 226,000 in 1967. Before it ended in October 1968, 643,000 tons of bombs were dropped on the North.[1] The air campaign had multiple purposes. It was designed to simultaneously deter North Vietnam from supporting the NLF insurgency in the South, increase the level of pain for doing so, interdict the flow of supplies to the South, assure the Saigon government of America's will to fight, and provide a bargaining mechanism to force negotiations. Strikes concentrated on transportation targets, such as railroads, bridges, roads, and vehicles, particularly along the Ho Chi Minh trail. In addition, Rolling Thunder destroyed 65 percent of the North's oil storage facilities and 59 percent of its power plants. As the leading student of the air war has concluded, "although bombing hindered the movement of men and supplies, it did not significantly affect infiltration." Nor did it deter the North or NLF from continuing to fight. Moreover, the air campaign was increasingly expensive. In 1965, it cost $6.60 to inflict $1.00 of damage in the North. The next year that cost rose to $9.60.[2]

The Johnson administration underestimated Hanoi's resilience and exaggerated the ability of the air war to influence the fighting in the south. Yet the military continued to advance unrealistic claims about the impact the bombing would have, and Rolling Thunder was continued long after its minimal success was known and some senior officials, most notably Secretary of Defense Robert McNamara, had concluded it was futile, because it was less expensive than troops, incurred fewer casualties than ground fighting, increased the cost of the war for the North, and seemed to offer, as the periodic bombing halts indicated, a bargaining chip in negotiations.[3] The war, however, would have to be won on the ground.

General Westmoreland's plan for victory was to grind down the enemy in a war of attrition and in the process demonstrate to the enemy that they could not win. At that point, they would no longer be willing to suffer the punishment being inflicted on them and would have to negotiate or quit. Success was measured by an increase in the "body count," that is, the number of enemy forces killed. The goal was to reach the so-called crossover point where NLF/North Vietnamese Army (NVA) losses exceeded their ability to replace those killed. When that happened, and the line on the graph of NLF/NVA casualties passed the line of numbers recruited, the enemy would begin to lose strength and face certain defeat. Through search and destroy missions, American commanders were confident they could find their opponents and use their superior firepower to inflict significant casualties. American forces would use the mobility their helicopters provided them to find the enemy and, with air and artillery support, overcome the difficult terrain, take the offensive, and obliterate the other side's ability to fight.

The escalation of the number of American troops was designed to carry out the three phases of the battle that Westmoreland saw as the route to victory. Phase I was to employ the nearly 200,000 troops sent in 1965 to halt the losing trend, prevent the collapse of Saigon, and disrupt NLF military efforts. The second phase was to be implemented in 1966 once the necessary infrastructure of bases and supplies was in place. Westmoreland saw this as the time to seize the initiative in the fighting by going on the offensive with the search and destroy operations. "If the enemy persisted, a period of a year to a year and a half following Phase II would be required for the defeat and destruction of the remaining enemy forces and base areas." Initially, the projections were to move into Phase III by 1967 and bring an end to the war prior to the 1968 election.[4] Based on McNamara's projection of 500 Americans killed per month, it was expected that American casualties would be around 18,000 killed. The secretary of defense informed Johnson that even though casualties would increase with escalation, and the war would not be won quickly, "the United States public will support this course of action" because it was designed "to bring about a favorable solution to the Vietnam problem."[5]

To implement this strategy, American forces were steadily increased over the next two and a half years, reaching 184,300 by the end of 1965, 385,300 on December 31, 1966, 448,800 by the middle of 1967, and 485,600 at the end of that year with a planned increase of over 40,000 troops in early 1968.[6] The first phase was successful as the arrival of American troops ended the series of military defeats the Army of the Republic of Vietnam (ARVN) was suffering and stabilized the Saigon regime. The NLF was denied a victory it would certainly have achieved without the intervention of the United States. As the war moved into 1966, however, the NLF and NVA matched American escalation with their own and adapted their tactics to survive the American onslaught. Most importantly, they used their knowledge of the terrain, support in the countryside, extensive tunnels, and base camps across the Cambodian and Laotian borders to offset the tremendous firepower of American forces, control the pace of the fighting, and limit the number of casualties they incurred.

As early as 1966, Department of Defense evaluations of the fighting indicated that the enemy initiated most of the engagements, and that less than 10 percent of the battles occurred because U.S. forces surprised an enemy unit. Furthermore, the majority of firefights in search and destroy operations came "as a surprise to the American tactical commander because the enemy is well-concealed and has been alerted." Summarizing the fighting through 1967, the National Security Council reported that "three-fourths of the battles are at the enemy's choice of time, place, type and duration," while the CIA reported that "less than one percent of nearly two million Allied small unit operations conducted in the last two years resulted in contact with the enemy."[7] Moreover, when the battles got too intense and casualties were taken too quickly, NLF/NVA forces would disengage, creating long lulls in the fighting.

This reality, along with the ineffectiveness of the bombing campaign and the consistent escalation of American forces with seemingly little progress, led to talk that the United States was locked in a bloody stalemate. A stalemate might have been enough except for two major problems. It could only produce success if there was a viable and legitimate government in Saigon that could eventually gain the allegiance of the population, and if the American public would tolerate a long, drawn-out, and indecisive war. The administration had cast the conflict as a just war of containment, necessary to defend America's national security in the global conflict with international communism, and one that protected American values and ideals in the battle with communist dictatorship. Constant escalation and an apparent stalemate, however, raised questions about the war and produced growing criticisms at home.

Early critics challenged the logic and rationale of the Johnson administration regarding the Vietnam War. The antiwar movement developed two fundamental and interrelated

critiques of the claim that it was a just war: that there was no
threat to the national interest in Vietnam, and that U.S. policy
and actions violated America's professed ideals and values.
Under the first category, dissenters rejected the seemingly
sacrosanct logic of containment and argued that there was no
such thing as monolithic communism, that the domino theory was not a realistic understanding of the complexities of
revolutionary movements and social change, and that it was
not a bipolar world. Vietnam, therefore, was not a pawn of
China. In fact, critics noted that Vietnam had a long history
of conflict with its neighbor to the north. Instead of serving
as an example of communist aggression, Vietnam was better
understood as a nation in the midst of a revolution and civil
war that had indigenous roots in the struggle against French
colonialism and seeking independence and self-determination.
The logic of containment, therefore, did not apply and no
fundamental American interests were at stake.

Relatedly, protesters saw the war as immoral and damaging to American values and institutions. The United States
was backing a military dictatorship in Saigon that lacked legitimacy; was corrupt, ineffective, and unpopular; and ruled
through force alone. This made the policy self-defeating in
the long run as it placed the United States in a position of
supporting a government without any base and created anti-
American sentiment in Vietnam and elsewhere. In addition,
the aid provided to South Vietnam made American moral arguments against communist regimes appear hypocritical
while at the same time violating American principles. Thus,
the costs in terms of soldiers killed and wounded, to the
economy and the Great Society programs, and in terms of
divisions at home, were not worth the sacrifice.

The antiwar movement was a complex, multifaceted effort that built on earlier peace groups and the civil rights and

student protests. The initial protests against the Vietnam War were small, limited to a few peace and student groups and some individual members of Congress, and had little impact on the administration's policy. Polls demonstrated wide-ranging approval of Johnson's decision to escalate and optimism about the course of the war, and protesters were dismissed as a radical fringe. With confidence in America's ability to defeat a guerrilla force in a small Third World nation, the administration seemingly had little reason to question McNamara's assurances of support for the fighting in Vietnam.

In early 1966, however, the Senate Foreign Relations Committee (SFRC) held public hearings on the war. Chaired by Senator J. William Fulbright, these meetings, and the nascent criticisms and debates over U.S. policy in Vietnam, provided legitimacy to the then struggling antiwar movement and established the parameters of the liberal, dove position on the war. The administration's critics on the committee argued that what was happening in Vietnam was part of a larger explosion of nationalist revolutions against colonialism throughout the Third World since the end of World War II and not due to some plot by Moscow to conquer the world, and warned that the United States could not police the world and should not attempt to block these revolutions. Moreover, they argued that Vietnam was not a primary concern for the United States, and rather than helping the fight against the Soviet Union, it was creating antipathy toward the United States as it was seen as acting arrogantly and as an imperial power.

Critics, therefore, dismissed the idea that it was a bipolar world, pointing to the disagreements between the Soviet Union and China as evidence that the communist world was not a monolithic mass. By supporting the regime in

Saigon, the United States was placing itself on the wrong side of the changes sweeping the world and damaging its long-term interests and relations with the Third World. In the process, in the words of Senator Frank Church, the United States had "downgrade[d] freedom by equating it with the absence of Communism; we upgrade a host of dictatorial regimes by dignifying them with membership in what we like to call the 'Free World.'" There were now many who questioned "our efforts in behalf of so many tottering governments afflicted by decadence and despotism and frequently despised by their own people."[8] Church, Fulbright, and others rejected the administration's arguments that the war was necessary to stop outside aggression in Vietnam. They saw the conflict in Vietnam as centered on the questions of independence and unity rather than communism and saw no reason why a revolution could not be both nationalist and led by communists.

Secretary of State Dean Rusk provided the standard responses to these criticisms. Testifying in a closed Executive Session of the Senate Foreign Relations Committee, he instructed the senators that they needed to recognize that there were two types of revolutions and to keep the "two different revolutions separate." The first was the "revolution of modernization, economic and social development, education." This type of revolution was occurring in South Vietnam and elsewhere, required stability, and justified American support and intervention. The other revolution was "the Communist world revolution . . . the dynamic force that concerns us all." This characterized the revolution in North Vietnam and had to be opposed because it and other communist states were totalitarian regimes hostile to the United States and freedom. Indeed, Rusk argued that the North saw the progress the South was making, that it was "being outstripped by the south," and had attacked in order to prevent Saigon's success.[9]

During the public hearings, Church and Rusk debated these points. Church asserted that revolutions were to be expected in the Third World as nations challenged the status quo to redress long-standing ills and to oust many of the tyrants the United States supported. The question was what would be the best policy for the United States in response to the revolutionary nationalism that was so prevalent in the world. "I gather," Church asked Rusk, "that wherever a revolution occurs against an established government, and that revolution, as most will doubtlessly be, will be infiltrated with Communists, that the United States regards it in its interests to prevent the success of Communist uprising." The senator found this to be a "self-defeating" policy and suggested a more nuanced understanding of the political changes in the world was necessary for the United States to cope with the "phenomena of revolt in the underdeveloped world." Rusk, however, did not budge from the axioms of the Cold War. He found a "fundamental difference between the kind of revolution which the Communists call their wars of national liberation, and the kind of revolution which is congenial to our own experience." The conflict in Vietnam stemmed from the actions of China, and this type of revolution "has nothing in common with the great American revolutionary tradition."[10]

Despite the doubts raised by individual senators and the questions raised by the hearings, antiwar opinion was slow to spread. Less than 25 percent of the population believed the United States had made a mistake in sending troops to Vietnam in 1965. At the beginning of 1967, this number had only grown to 30 percent as a sizeable majority continued to support the war. Yet by the fall of that year antiwar opinion broke out of the confines of the campuses and traditional peace groups and spread throughout American society. The continued increase in American forces and casualties in what appeared to be a military stalemate and growing legitimacy of opposition to the administration, along with the first signs of economic problems due to the war, led to this dramatic shift in popular opinion. The seemingly inconclusive nature of the fighting with no appreciable changes in over two years also led to the development of a growing credibility gap and skepticism about the administration's claims of progress and the necessity of the war in the face of other evidence, most notably the constant need for escalation, growing casualty lists, and eyewitness accounts by soldiers and reporters. The broad-based nature of the antiwar sentiment was demonstrated in October when polls showed that for the first time a plurality of Americans thought the war was mistake by a margin of 46 to 44 percent.[11]

Optimism in Saigon

If the war was a stalemate, as many observers and critics now claimed, then it was almost certain that support for the war would continue to drop. If that happened, it was sure to further divide the nation and have negative consequences on Johnson's chances for reelection. There was now a critical disjuncture between the administration and a sizeable portion of the population over the importance of the war to the United States and its security, and the success of the American military effort. At the same time that the support for the war dropped significantly, officials in Vietnam rejected the analysis that the war was a stalemate and reported to

Washington that while it was slower coming than initially expected, definite progress was being made in defeating the enemy on the battlefield and turning Saigon into a viable government, and that the war was being won. The way they measured progress—elections held, body count, kill ratios, and villages pacified—proved to them that the strategy of attrition was working and that the application of American force was having the desired impact. American troops were wearing the enemy down and building Saigon up, and the end was coming into sight.

Ambassador Ellsworth Bunker reported to Rusk in late August that "progress in the war has been steady on all fronts. We can defeat the enemy by patient, continued, and concerted effort." He stated that the military campaign, the pacification programs in the countryside, and the political efforts to improve the performance of the Saigon government were all interrelated, and all had "steadily improved since the spring of 1965." Notably, the war was going well, and "recruiting by the VC in the South is increasingly difficult and has fallen off by about half," making it more a North Vietnamese war as military operations and pacification programs impaired the ability of the NLF to fight effectively. In addition, there were now a constitution and elections that made Nguyen Van Thieu the president and Nguyen Cao Ky the vice president of South Vietnam. Together, they were bringing political stability and a government "which has a more widely accepted mandate and is thus in a stronger position." In conclusion, Bunker noted that "now that the initiative is ours and the enemy is beginning to hurt, maximum pressure must be maintained."[12]

Bunker's report reflected the consensus of all senior American officials in Saigon. Westmoreland reported on August 29 that "enemy losses have increased 53% from 8,411 per month in FY 66 to 12,782 per month in FY 67," were continuing to increase, and now exceeded their ability to replace these troops.[13] What made these numbers most significant for Westmoreland was that it was only in the last year that U.S. forces had the capacity "to apply real pressure on the enemy" and to start "grinding down the guerrilla forces." Prior to that, his troops were tied up preventing the collapse of Saigon and developing the physical facilities required to support the soldiers. In the first year, he had half of all his forces working in logistic support. Now, "of every 5 men I receive I will augment logistic support by 1 man and 4 can be deployed in a combat role."[14]

As Military Assistance Command, Vietnam (MACV) summarized their evaluation, "North Vietnam is paying a tremendous price for its aggression, with nothing to show in return. South Vietnam, despite continued suffering and trails, is making progress on all fronts—military, political, and economic. The war is by no means over but neither is it stalemated. We are steadily winning it, and the pace accelerates as we reinforce our successes and intensify our pressures."[15] General Harold Johnson, Army chief of staff, also dismissed the idea of a stalemate and claimed that the United States was making progress "on all fronts." While communist forces were on the offensive when the United States arrived in 1965, they were now on the defensive, being "sought out and hammered relentlessly," unable to replace their losses or sustain any attacks. "Those facts do not add up to a stalemate in my book," he declared.[16]

Central to the claims of progress were the optimistic reports on pacification coming out of Saigon. Robert Komer, head of the Civilian Operations and Revolutionary Development Support program (CORDS), reported to Bunker that increased "*military success against enemy main forces has permitted pacification to get underway again.*" He claimed that as of September 1967, "68% of the SVN population [was] living under reasonably secure conditions," while only 17 percent were still under NLF control. The rest lived in contested areas. Moreover, the pacification program, after just one year, was still "gathering movement forward" and "should achieve substantially greater results in 1968."[17]

Director of the CIA Richard Helms presented all of this information to the cabinet on October 4. Armed with charts that showed steady military progress and growing success in the pacification program, Helms concluded that "Hanoi knows that the war in the South is going against them." Most telling was the falloff in the number of enemy casualties and the number of battles in the last few months. This decline was taken as an indication that they were losing strength and could no longer take the initiative on the battlefield. At another meeting, National Security Advisor Walt Whitman Rostow, using similar statistics prepared by MACV, outlined a picture of a defeated enemy that was losing men and the ability to fight. Rostow noted that "statistics cannot give you everything 100%, but they can and do confirm progress."[18] The next month, the CIA reported that "manpower is a major problem confronting the Communists. Losses have been increasing and recruitment in South Vietnam is becoming more difficult," the strength of the enemy had "declined in the last year," and the "overall strength and effectiveness of the military forces and the political infrastructure will continue to decline." The communist strategy, and only hope, was to try and "sustain a protracted war of attrition" to persuade the United States to pull out or reach an agreement on Hanoi's terms.[19]

Given this analysis, Bunker informed Washington that the embassy in Saigon planned to demonstrate to the press and public "that we are making solid progress and are not in a stalemate." Central to the argument refuting the idea of a stalemate was that the "enemy is fast losing control of the people for his side, his recruitment has dropped off sharply, he is having food shortages, and he is having serious problems collecting VC taxes." Due to the fact that "our first year [of fighting] was spent primarily on logistical build-up," the progress made was seen as even greater than it appeared. "Enemy strength in South Vietnam has declined over the past year," Bunker concluded, as the "the number of troops infiltrated and recruited by the enemy over the last six months has not been as great as his deaths, desertions, and other losses." Estimates provided by MACV stated that whereas in the first quarter of 1966 enemy strength was growing (7,000 recruits and 12,000 infiltrated from the North versus 8,300 casualties) by over 10,000 troops, in the third quarter of 1967 it was declining (3,100 recruits and 6,000 infiltrated versus 12,000 casualties) by 2,900, along with the number of battles it could fight. This trend led to the "weakening, at least at the lower level, of the enemy's will, especially the southern VC," a "declining ability to recruit in South Vietnam," and an inability "to mount a major offensive." All this data was reflected in the successes of the pacification program where "approximately 70 percent" of the population was under the control of the Saigon government and nearly 75 percent of the people participated in recent elections.[20]

Using this information, MACV informed reporters in Saigon that the fighting ability of the enemy was declining and the war was being won. The military command were "all very optimistic. We see this situation getting steadily better" and predicted that by 1968 the enemy was "going to be in very bad shape." General Bruce Palmer said that "the Viet

Cong has been defeated from Da Nang all the way down in the populated areas. He can't get food and he can't recruit. He has been forced to change his strategy from trying to control the people on the coast to trying to survive in the mountains." After being briefed in Saigon, Vice President Hubert Humphrey stated that "we are beginning to win this struggle. We are on the offensive. Territory is being gained. We are making steady progress."[21]

Thus, administration officials faced a paradox that they did not understand. All of the reports from Vietnam, all the analysis, all of the statistics, indicated an ever-increasing improvement of the situation on all fronts. Yet at the same time, popular support for the war was steadily declining. General Omar Bradley, who was in Saigon that fall, set out the dilemma upon his return to Washington. He told Rostow that "he emerged with a sense of great optimism," was impressed with the military performance, and stated that "there is not the slightest doubt in his mind that the war is not stalemated. We are moving forward." In summary, Rostow informed Johnson, Bradley was "convinced that we were well on the way to winning the war." Yet all of this could be lost. The main "problem was to keep a base of public support in the United States for the effort in Viet Nam." If that was lost, then the United States would not have the time to achieve victory.[22]

THE WISE MEN

With the war now in its third year and the confidence of the public in the endeavor slipping, President Johnson decided to consult with the so-called Wise Men of American foreign policy to discuss this paradox. The president wanted the opinions of this bipartisan group of leading statesmen on whether there was anything he should be doing in Vietnam that he was not at present to achieve his goals and to find out what suggestions they had "to rally and unite our own people behind the effort in Vietnam." The group that met on November 1–2 consisted of former Secretary of State Dean Acheson, George Ball, General Bradley, McGeorge Bundy, the attorneys Clark Clifford and Arthur Dean, former Secretary of the Treasury C. Douglas Dillon, Associate Supreme Court Justice Abe Fortas, Ambassador Averill Harriman, Henry Cabot Lodge, former State Department official Robert Murphy, and General Maxwell Taylor. On Wednesday evening, November 1, there were two briefings on the situation in Vietnam by General Earle Wheeler, chairman of the Joint Chiefs of Staff, and George Carver, assistant to CIA Director Richard Helms on Vietnam. Rostow described

Meeting of the Wise Men, November 2, 1967. Clockwise from head of table, Richard Helms, George Ball, Nicholas Katzenbach, Dean Rusk, Walt Rostow (seated in background), President Lyndon B. Johnson, Robert McNamara, Douglas Dillon, McGeorge Bundy, Arthur Dean, Henry Cabot Lodge, Robert Murphy, Dean Acheson, Omar Bradley, Maxwell Taylor, Clark Clifford.

the briefings as "impressive," and told the president that Carver had "hit just the right balance between the progress we have made and the problems we still confront." The main points of the reports were "that there was very great progress since 1965" in Vietnam, that the United States and South Vietnam controlled the future, and that Hanoi's leaders "would make a strategic decision to end the war when they had decided the U.S. would not behave like the French did in 1954 and when a viable state structure seemed on the way to emerging in Saigon."[23]

These optimistic reports were supported by a letter sent by Ambassador Bunker to Secretary of State Rusk on his six months in Saigon. Bunker noted steady improvement throughout 1967, claiming the military was now on the offensive, that pacification was a "success equalling [sic] in importance the military improvements," and that the training and performance of the ARVN had "improved considerably." In particular, Bunker pointed toward village and hamlet programs under the Civilian Operations and Revolutionary Development Support program as making real strides in winning the war.[24] Reportedly, almost 70 percent of the South Vietnamese population was pacified and under the control of the Saigon government. Combined with the military's reports that the war of attrition was working and that the crossover point had been reached where the enemy could no longer replace its losses, victory was said to be within reach.[25]

The next day the Wise Men met with President Johnson and senior administration officials, including William Bundy, Helms, McNamara, Rostow, and Rusk. Prior to the meeting, Rostow reported to Johnson that there was no support for negotiations in the group and "no sentiment for our pulling out of Vietnam."[26] Johnson said he wanted to "know if our course in Vietnam was right," and if not, what should be done. In addition, he noted that he was "deeply concerned about the deterioration of public support and the lack of editorial support for our policies" and wanted to know "how do we unite the country?" Based on the information they were presented the previous day, all agreed that the situation had improved in Vietnam, great progress was being made, and the United States had to maintain its current policy and press on with the war. It was necessary to uphold containment, keep international communism at bay, and maintain American credibility. They, therefore, had no recommendations for changes. Acheson noted that he thought the war was "going well," and that he was "encouraged by the ground fighting in the South and that we are taking the initiative. I got the impression this is a matter we can and will win." Ball declared that the reports they received were "very reassuring" that the "war of attrition and civil action is in competent hands and we are doing very well there."[27]

The group was unanimous in opposing any idea that the United States should get out of Vietnam. Acheson said "absolutely not," while Bundy stated it was "as impossible as it is undesirable." They also opposed any idea of new efforts at negotiations on the basis that there was nothing to be gained. The consensus was that you cannot negotiate with communists. Acheson claimed that the Korean War did not end by negotiations. "When these fellows decide they can't defeat the South, then they will give up. This is the way it was in Korea. This is the way the Communists operate." Moreover, further talk about negotiations just encouraged the enemy and would be interpreted by Hanoi "as a sign of weakness and would make the Communists believe they are winning the battle for public opinion."[28]

Secretary of Defense Robert McNamara and Dean Acheson, November 2, 1967.

What the Wise Men did recommend to the president was more and better communication with the nation on the progress that was being made in Vietnam. Bundy argued that the successes had to be explained to the American people. "What is eroding public support," Bundy stated, "are the battles and deaths and dangers to the sons of mothers and fathers with no picture of a result in sight." The emphasis and discussion had to be shifted to the "light at the end of the tunnel" instead of the fighting; the policy was bringing about "results and the end of the road." Others agreed and encouraged the president to bring Bunker and Westmoreland back from Vietnam to explain the progress of the war to the nation. As Clifford stated, "an effort must be made to explain and to educate the American people," and the best people to do that are the ones in Vietnam who have the first-hand knowledge. He also cautioned Johnson that he had to remember that most American wars, except World War II, were unpopular at some point with large numbers of people, and "that no matter what this accomplishes, this will not be a popular war." Still, Johnson had to continue the war "because what we are doing is right. But recognizing this fact, I hope we won't get frustrated."[29]

It was clear, Clifford stated in conclusion, that "other nations say we have provided them with a shield. They cannot depend upon the British or the French. This has been an enormous success but we won't be able to convince the American people of that as long as it is going on. So we should go right on doing what we're going to do. . . . Any cessation in the South or the North will be interpreted as a sign of weakness of the American people. If we keep up the pressure on them, gradually the will of the Viet Cong and the North Vietnamese will wear down."[30] In short, the Wise Men informed Johnson that the United States was indeed winning the war, but that he had a public relations problem as this news was not reaching the American public. Rostow picked up on this point, agreeing with Clifford that "this will not be a popular war," but that the progress being made would win back support and "that there are ways of guiding the press to show light at the end of the tunnel." It was a matter of staying the course to demonstrate the soundness of the strategy and the correctness of the policy. Concluding the meeting, Johnson stated that the U.S. presence in Vietnam was achieving success in the country and in the whole region. It had "hampered China's policy and caused reversals against China in Indonesia and other parts of the world. Practically all the leaders in Asia are in deep sympathy with us."[31] This alone was justification enough to continue the war.

That night, Johnson held a dinner for House Democrats where he appraised them of his meeting earlier in the day. He acknowledged that "our people are terrifically distressed and disturbed about Vietnam" due to rising casualties and are wondering why the administration cannot "find some way to get out of this mess." The only route out was to continue to apply military pressure, and he assured them that everyone knew that "Ho Chi Minh is not going to win this." There could be no negotiations at this point because it "does nothing except mislead the Communists and make them think that we are weaker instead of stronger." He did not know exactly how long the enemy could hold up, but even in the face of defeat they would not negotiate. "The Communists don't negotiate," Johnson declared. "They just decide to quit some day."[32]

Johnson asked Bundy at the conclusion of the Wise Men's meeting to provide him with a summary of their key recommendations and his own thoughts and suggestions. Bundy reiterated the group's support of Johnson's policy and actions in Vietnam and the rejection of a pursuit of negotiations. The best advice Bundy had for the president was "to keep calm" and stay the course. He acknowledged that "public discontent with the war is now wide and deep," and that "one of the few things that helps us right now is public distaste for the violent doves." Still, "people are getting fed up with the endlessness of the fighting," and it was that and "the cost of the war in lives and money, coupled with the lack of light at the end of the tunnel," not the doves' arguments, that was causing a loss of support. Only seeing progress would turn that around.[33]

The End Comes into View

Instinctively, Johnson knew Bundy was correct and decided to bring Westmoreland, Bunker, and Komer back to Washington in mid-November to explain to the nation the status of the war and the progress being made. The president hoped that this public relations blitz would reverse the direction of the polls and shore up support for the war going into the election year. General Westmoreland set the tone for this public relations campaign upon his arrival at Andrews Air Force Base outside of Washington, DC, on November 15. He told waiting reporters that he was "very, very encouraged" by recent developments. "We are making real progress. Everybody is very optimistic that I know of who is intimately associated with the effort there." He described as "absolutely inaccurate" a statement that recent battles indicated that the enemy had the initiative on the battlefield, declaring that "we have beat them to the punch every time."[34]

Two days later, in his first interview, he indicated that he thought American forces could begin to withdraw "within two years or less." His optimism was based on the course of the battles, the number of enemy killed passing the crossover point of their ability to replace those losses, the increasing number of enemy defectors, and the percentage of the population brought under Saigon's control. In Saigon, he noted, "the consensus is that the enemy is being weakened and our side is growing stronger." This was not just true of American commanders, but "also evident from captured documents and from interrogations of defectors and prisoners-of-war. There is evidence that the enemy is beginning to realize that he cannot win." Westmoreland rejected any notion that the war was a stalemate, stating that "stalemate implies a lack of progress and such is not the case in Vietnam. We are making steady and real progress on all fronts." The enemy, the general concluded, did not have inexhaustible resources and was suffering from manpower shortages, "having great difficulty recruiting the guerrillas that he needs." American firepower was "beginning to take its toll" on enemy forces and morale, and the United States would "progressively from now on . . . weaken the enemy by virtue of the pressure that hopefully we will continue to apply."[35]

On NBC's *Meet the Press*, Westmoreland was even more specific, rejecting the idea of a stalemate and declaring that "we are winning a war of attrition now." The body count was up, Westmoreland assured the reporters, while the enemy could no longer replace those killed, and the remaining forces were "only about 55 percent combat effective." As to the question of why he would need more troops if there was

National Security Advisor Walt Whitman Rostow briefing President Johnson and members of Congress, November 16, 1967.

so much progress, the general argued that it was "a sound strategic principle to reenforce success," and that the time was optimum "to reenforce this success with troop augmentations." The larger force would allow him to "continue to grind down the enemy" and secure South Vietnam within two years.[36] This time line was adopted, Westmoreland told his staff, because it "straddles the Presidential elections of November '68 implying the election is not a bench mark from a military point of view."[37]

This optimism was not just for public consumption. Bunker and Westmoreland told the president, Joint Chiefs of Staff, and Congress the same things. The ambassador reported to Johnson that there was "steady progress on the political, military, and economic front in South Vietnam," particularly in nation building and rural pacification projects. Enemy military efforts were now designed to achieve some dramatic victory and draw forces away from the pacification effort, a shift that served as an acknowledgment of their declining fortunes.[38] Westmoreland repeated all of the optimistic reports and analysis produced in Saigon over the past few months in his meeting with the Joint Chiefs of Staff. He declared that the NLF "guerrilla forces have undergone serious attrition" and were only able to recruit half as many men as a year earlier, and that the North's main forces "are being driven into the border areas without seriously weakening our military forces in the populated areas." Moreover, the enemy could no longer replace their losses, and U.S. forces would "progressively weaken the enemy" to a point where it would be possible to turn the war over to Saigon in two years or less.[39]

In a briefing with congressional leaders, the commander of U.S. forces in Vietnam boldly stated that "we are confident that we are winning this war." Progress was not always easy to see, "but by every means of measuring this progress that I have been able to devise . . . I am confident that we are grinding this enemy down." As he told the president earlier, it was his opinion "that in two years or less . . . the enemy will be so weakened and our allies, the South Vietnamese, will be sufficiently strong that we will be able to progressively reduce the level or our commitment." Prompted by President Johnson to give his opinion on the idea that the United States was "bogged down into a stalemate," Westmoreland replied that "this stalemate thesis is complete fiction." There was no question in his mind that steady progress was being made and that the enemy realized they could not win. The NLF/NVA was getting desperate for some victory, but "he has struck out on every occasion." Their only hope was a loss of U.S. will to finish the war. Westmoreland concluded by saying that the key to victory at this point was "endurance on the battlefield, and patience at home."[40]

Robert Komer briefing President Johnson in the Oval Office, November 16, 1967.

Robert Komer was the most optimistic and specific, reporting to the president that as long as the United States kept up "pressure on the North, I am more convinced than ever that by mid-1968 at the latest it will be clear to everyone that we are 'winning' the military war."[41] He later recalled that they had "reported confidently to the President that 'Boss, finally all this stuff you have given us is beginning to pay off, and we look forward to 1968 as a big year of success for us.'" He continued:

> we were not engaging in deception. We genuinely believed at the end of 1967 that we were getting on top. . . . Westmoreland believed, Abrams believed, Bunker believed, and I believed that finally, with five hundred thousand goddamn troops and all that air, and pacification finally getting underway, with the Vietnamese having set up a constitution and elections, we really were winning. We couldn't quite see clearly how soon, but this wasn't public relations, this wasn't Lyndon Johnson telling us to put a face on it. We genuinely thought we were making it.[42]

The public relations campaign culminated on November 21 with Westmoreland's speech to the National Press Club. "I am absolutely certain," he declared, "that whereas in 1965 the enemy was winning, today he is certainly losing. There are indications that the Viet Cong and even Hanoi may know this." Yet Hanoi was probably "operating from the delusion that political pressure here combined with the tactical defeat of a major unit might force the US to 'throw in the towel.'" Only this hope explained why they were continuing the war. Westmoreland confidently predicted that Phase II of the war would be completed by the end of the year and "with 1968, a new phase is now starting. We have reached an important point where the end begins to come into view." He emphatically concluded that "*we are* making

General William C. Westmoreland briefing President Johnson in the Oval Office, November 16, 1967.

progress." Victory "lies within our grasp—the enemy's hopes are dim. With your support we will give you a success that will impact not only on South Vietnam, but on every emerging nation in the world."[43]

Westmoreland and Bunker had done everything the president had asked in order "to get a better story to the American people" because they fully believed what they were saying.[44] They had painted a picture that the tide of the war had favorably changed with the United States achieving its military and political goals. The enemy could not replace its losses, mount an offensive, or challenge American forces. In addition, Saigon now controlled most of the population in the South and was gaining strength on a daily basis. Victory, in brief, was in sight. There was a "light at the end of the tunnel." All that was needed was the time to complete the job. Yet all of their positive evaluations and optimism barely changed the public's view of the war. The percentage of respondents who believed the war was a mistake only dropped one point, from 46 to 45, while those who supported the effort rose by just two points to 46 percent.[45]

What the public and the Wise Men did not know was that Secretary of Defense McNamara had also reached the conclusion that the war was a stalemate. He, therefore, sought to change the direction of American policy. His advice ran completely counter to what Johnson heard from the Wise Men and his other senior advisors. Writing to the president on November 1, McNamara stated that he now believed that the "continuation of our present course of action in Southeast Asia would be dangerous, costly in lives, and unsatisfactory to the American people." If escalation continued, it would not bring about significant enough progress by the end of 1968 to prevent the "continued erosion of popular support for our involvement in Vietnam." He stated that "neither the additional troops now scheduled nor augmentation of our forces by a much greater amount holds great promise of bringing the North Vietnamese and Viet Cong forces visibly closer to collapse during the next 15 months." That would mean that "as the months go by, there will be both increasing pressure for widening the war and continued loss of support for American participation in the struggle. . . . There is," McNamara concluded, "a very real question whether under these circumstances it will be possible to maintain our efforts in South Vietnam for the necessary time to accomplish our objectives there."[46]

In order to keep the war politically viable, he recommended a "stabilization of our military effort" and a "halt in the bombing of the North." The capping of escalation, McNamara argued, "would help convince Hanoi that we are prepared to stay in Vietnam as long as necessary" and "increase support for the war at home by removing anxiety about possible increases in our activity," while the bombing halt would also increase support and provide the possibility for negotiations to begin.[47] McNamara had already concluded that the bombing was having no positive impact on the war. In testimony to the Senate, he noted that the cost of Rolling Thunder to the United States was three times greater than the amount of damage inflicted, that the bombing only stopped about 2 percent of Northern troops from reaching the South, and that more supplies than ever were making their way down the Ho Chi Minh trail.[48] The secretary of defense, therefore, was willing to suspend the air war in an effort to get talks started to end the conflict.

Johnson asked Rostow to solicit the input of other senior officials on McNamara's ideas without indicating who made the proposal. To a person, they rejected its central recommendations. For example, Bunker and Westmoreland opposed a bombing halt on military grounds and argued that there was no evidence it would lead to negotiations, while Westmoreland added that it would be "foolish" to announce a capping of American forces.[49] Rostow joined Rusk in similarly rejecting the logic of McNamara's argument, finding that "a unilateral bombing cessation and an announced policy of 'stabilization' would . . . be judged in Hanoi a mark of weakness rather than evidence of increased U.S. capacity to sweat out the war." The "evidence of solid progress" was becoming increasingly clear, and this was not the time to change policy.[50]

Clark Clifford's response best summarized the views from the recent meeting of the Wise Men and other senior officials. He told Johnson that the course of action recommended would "retard the possibility of concluding the conflict rather than accelerating it." The enemy was continuing the war when it was evident it had no chance of winning because "Hanoi is depending upon a weakening of the will of the United States to carry on the war. Their previous experience with the French has convinced them that the same result will occur again insofar as the United States is concerned." The war will never end "if they think our determination is lessening. On the other hand, if our pressure is unremitting and their losses continue to grow, and hope fades for any sign of weakening on our part, then some day they will conclude that the game is not worth the candle." Stabilization and a bombing halt, therefore, were the worst possible courses of action. Clifford asked: "Would the unconditional suspension of the bombing, without any effort to extract a quid pro quo persuade Hanoi that we are firm and unyielding in our conviction to force them to desist from their aggressive designs? The answer is a loud and resounding 'no'" Instead, "it would be interpreted by Hanoi as (a) evidence of our discouragement and frustration, and (b) an admission of the wrongness and immorality of our bombing of the North, and (c) the first step in our ultimate total disengagement from the conflict." Similarly an announcement of a capping of escalation would bring "chortles of unholy glee" from Hanoi, destroying any bargaining position the United States held.[51]

Clifford concluded by invoking the central logic of containment and the necessity of the war in Vietnam. He noted that the "future of our children and grandchildren require" the war be ended "by accomplishing our purpose, i.e., the thwarting of the aggression by North Vietnam, aided by China and Russia." The stakes, therefore, were too high for such a risky gamble as stabilization and a bombing halt posed. Moreover, "free peoples everywhere, and Communists everywhere, in fact the entire world, is watching to see if the United States meant what it said when it announced its intention to help defend South Vietnam." It was critical that American credibility be upheld and that other nations respect the United States. "It is clear to me," Clifford noted in his last line, "that the course of action offered in the memorandum does not accomplish this purpose."[52]

In contrast to McNamara's proposal, Secretary of State Rusk provided a year-end summary of the optimistic appraisal of the war to all U.S. embassies in the world. The points he outlined were to be used by ambassadors with their host governments and other diplomats. The central point was that the United States and South Vietnam "are

President Lyndon Johnson in Cam Rahn Bay, December 23, 1967, pinning medals on American soldiers.

making substantial progress" in the war. This was most evident by the comparison of 1965 to 1967. When U.S. forces first arrived, the enemy was "decimating South Vietnamese forces." Now, the situation had "clearly been reversed," with kill ratios up and communist forces declining in strength, unable to replace their losses and incapable of mounting a large-scale offensive. All this meant that Saigon was more in control of the nation than ever before and steadily bringing more of the population under its protection.[53]

On this basis, Johnson rejected McNamara's proposals and held to the optimistic accounts of the war that officials in Saigon were providing. He concluded that "a unilateral and unrequited bombing stand-down would be read in both Hanoi and the United States as a sign of weakening will." A "so-called policy of stabilization" of ground forces would have the same political impact.[54] With McNamara's views now so out of step with those of other top officials, Johnson announced on November 28 that McNamara would be stepping down as secretary of defense to become the head of the World Bank at the end of February and that Clifford would succeed him at the Pentagon. A leading Washington attorney, pillar of the foreign policy establishment, and presidential advisor since Truman, Clifford had consistently supported the war, and Johnson took great comfort in his backing of American policy. There would be no change of course.

In a quick visit to Vietnam right before Christmas, Johnson told the gathered Senior Unit Commanders that the United States was "not going to yield. We are not going to shimmy."[55] While presenting Distinguished Service Medals to Generals Westmoreland, Bruce Palmer, Creighton Abrams, and others, and Medals of Freedom to Ambassador Bunker and Komer, Johnson stated that in Vietnam, "all the challenges have been met. The enemy is not beaten but he knows

General William C. Westmoreland, President Johnson, and Ambassador Ellsworth Bunker, December 23, 1967, Cam Rahn Bay.

that he has met his master in the field."[56] The NLF was desperately trying to hold on, hoping America's will would falter. That would not happen, Johnson promised. The United States would fight until the mission was accomplished.

The news, the president believed, was getting better. The worst of the days of trial were seemingly behind him. As he stated on New Year's Day 1968, "we feel that the enemy knows that he can no longer win a military victory in South Vietnam." In his State of the Union message on January 17, 1968, Johnson declared that the enemy continued to "hope that America's will to persevere can be broken. Well—he is wrong. America will persevere. Our patience and our perseverance will match our power. Aggression will never prevail."[57] Nineteen Sixty-Eight, the president thought, would be the year of victory in Vietnam.

NOTES

1. Robert Anthony Pape, *Bombing to Win: Air Power and Coercion in War* (Ithaca: Cornell University Press, 1996), 185.

2. Mark Clodfelter, *The Limits of Air Power: The American Bombing of North Vietnam* (New York: Free Press, 1989), 134.

3. On McNamara's doubts see, McNamara to Johnson, November 1, 1967, Gibbons Papers, Box 32, LBJL.

4. James William Gibson, *The Perfect War: The War We Couldn't Lose and How We Did* (New York: Vintage, 1986), 94–97.

5. McNamara, Memorandum for the President, July 1, 1965, NSF: NSC Meeting File, Box 1, LBJL.

6. George Donelson Moss, *Vietnam: An American Ordeal*, 3rd ed. (Upper Saddle River, NJ: Prentice Hall, 1998), 446.

7. Gibson, *The Perfect War*, 108–09.

8. Frank Church, "How Many Dominican Republics and Vietnams Can We Take On?," *New York Times Magazine*, November 28, 1965, 44–45, 177–78.

9. *Executive Sessions, 1964*, XVI:195–96.

10. J. William Fulbright, ed., *The Vietnam Hearings* (New York: Vintage, 1966), 52–54.

11. *Gallup Opinion Index, Report No. 33* (Princeton: Gallup International, 1968), 5; George Gallup, *The Gallup Poll: Public Opinion 1935–1971*, Vol. III (New York: Random House, 1971), 2010–87.

12. Bunker to Rusk, August 26, 1967, Gibbons Papers, Box 29, LBJL.

13. Westmoreland to Clifford and Taylor, "Achievement of Objective," August 29, 1967, Gibbons Papers, Box 29, LBJL.

14. "Substance of General Westmoreland's Opening Remarks to the JCS," November 17, 1967, Gibbons Papers, Box 32, LBJL.

15. "Presentation on the Vietnam War by the Military Adviser, United States," October 26, 1967, NSF: CO Vietnam, Box 99, LBJL.

16. Johnson, Speech before the Defense Orientation Conference, September 29, 1967, NSF: CO Vietnam, Box 103 LBJL.

17. Komer to Bunker, October 1, 1967, Westmoreland Papers, Box 14, LBJL (emphasis in the original).

18. Cabinet Meeting, October 4, 1967, Cabinet Papers, Box 10, and November 15, 1967, Cabinet Papers, Box 11, LBJL.

19. NIE, "Capabilities of the Vietnamese Communists for Fighting in South Vietnam," November 13, 1967, Gibbons Papers, Box 32, LBJL.

20. Bunker to Rusk, October 7, 1967, NSF: CO Vietnam, Box 99, LBJL.

21. Don Oberdorfer, *TET!* (New York: Avon Books, 1971), 119–20.

22. Memorandum of Conversation, Rostow, September 9, 1967, Gibbons Papers, Box 30, LBJL.

23. Rostow to Johnson, November 2, 1967, Johnson Papers, Meeting Notes File, Box 2, LBJL.

24. Jones to Johnson, November 2, 1967, Johnson Papers, Meeting Notes File, Box 2, LBJL.

25. Marilyn Young, *The Vietnam Wars, 1945–1990* (New York: HarperCollins, 1991), 213–14.

26. Rostow to Johnson, November 2, 1967, Johnson Papers, Meeting Notes File, Box 2, LBJL.

27. Jones to Johnson, November 2, 1967, Johnson Papers, Meeting Notes File, Box 2, LBJL.

28. Jones to Johnson, November 2, 1967, Johnson Papers, Meeting Notes File, Box 2, LBJL.

29. Jones to Johnson, November 2, 1967, Johnson Papers, Meeting Notes File, Box 2, LBJL.

30. Jones to Johnson, November 2, 1967, Johnson Papers, Meeting Notes File, Box 2, LBJL.

31. Jones to Johnson, November 2, 1967, Johnson Papers, Meeting Notes File, Box 2, LBJL.

32. Transcript, "Stag Dinner for House Members," November 2, 1967, Congressional Briefings on Vietnam, Box 1, LBJL.

33. Bundy to Johnson, November 10, 1967, President's Appointment File, Box 81, LBJL.

34. Westmoreland Interviewed by the Press, November 15, 1967, Westmoreland Papers, Box 14, LBJL.

35. "Interview with General William C. Westmoreland, USA, and Steve Rowan, CBS," November 17, 1967, Westmoreland Papers, Box 14, LBJL.

36. Transcript, *Meet the Press*, November 19, 1967, Westmoreland Papers, Box 14, LBJL.

37. Quoted in Oberdorfer, *TET!*, 123.

38. Johnson to Johnson, November 16, 1967, Gibbons Papers, Box 32, LBJL.

39. "Substance of General Westmoreland's Opening Remarks to the JCS," November 17, 1967, Gibbons Papers, Box 32, LBJL.

40. Congressional Briefing, November 16, 1967, Congressional Briefings on Vietnam, Box 1, LBJL.

41. Komer to Johnson, October 4, 1967, NSF: Memos to the President, Rostow, Box 23, LBJL.

42. Quoted in Kim Willlenson, *The Bad War: An Oral History of the Vietnam War* (New York: New American Library, 1987), 95–97.

43. Westmoreland, "Vietnam War Progress Report," November 21, 1967, Westmoreland Papers, Box 14, LBJL (emphasis in the original).

44. Johnson to Johnson, November 16, 1967, Gibbons Papers, Box 32, LBJL.

45. Gallup, *The Gallup Poll*, Vol. III, 2099.

46. McNamara to Johnson, November 1, 1967, Gibbons Papers, Box 32, LBJL.

47. McNamara to Johnson, November 1, 1967, Gibbons Papers, Box 32, LBJL.

48. Oberdorfer, *TET!*, 113-14.

49. Rostow to Johnson, November 20, 1967, and November 21, 1967, NSF: Memos to the President, Rostow, Box 25, LBJL.

50. Rostow to Johnson, November 2, 1967, Gibbons Papers, Box 32, LBJL.

51. Clifford Memorandum, November 7, 1967, NSF: Memos to the President, Rostow, Box 25, LBJL.

52. Clifford Memorandum, November 7, 1967, NSF: Memos to the President, Rostow, Box 25, LBJL.

53. Rusk to Diplomatic Posts, December 8, 1967, NSF: CO Vietnam, Box 100, LBJL.

54. Memorandum of President for the File, December 18, 1967, Gibbons Papers, Box 33, LBJL.

55. *Public Papers of the Presidents: Johnson 1967*, II (Washington, DC: Government Printing Office, 1968), 1183.

56. *Public Papers of the Presidents: Johnson 1967*, II, 1186.

57. *Public Papers of the Presidents: Johnson 1968-69*, I (Washington, DC: Government Printing Office, 1970), 2, 25.

Chapter Three

THE TET OFFENSIVE

T HE TET OFFENSIVE CHANGED THE COURSE OF THE
war. On January 30, 1968, the beginning of the Tet holiday,
approximately 84,000 NLF and NVA forces launched nearly
simultaneous attacks against over 100 cities and military installations in South Vietnam. The assaults on the capital of
Saigon and provincial and district capitals from the Demilitarized Zone (DMZ) to the Mekong Delta caught American
commanders by surprise. That it was so large, well coordinated, and aimed at the cities was completely unexpected as
it contradicted all of the key assumptions of American leaders about the war and their optimistic reports in the fall. Tet,
the Vietnamese lunar New Year, is the most sacred of Vietnamese holidays, a time of family feasts and celebrations. It
was also an annual period of cease-fire in the war, and half
of the Army of the Republic of Vietnam's (ARVN) troops
were on leave when the attacks came, adding to the element
of surprise and the impact of the Tet Offensive.

The largest and most important battle of the war up
to this point, and the first to be fought in the cities, the Tet
Offensive's importance goes beyond its military aspects to

its political, psychological, and economic impact in the United States. It was a perfect illustration of the U.S. war effort for two reasons. First, American forces, with their overwhelming firepower, inflicted enormous casualties on the enemy as they beat back the attacks and proved that they could frustrate the enemy militarily, deny it control of the cities, and continue to prop up the Saigon regime. On the negative side, all the United States appeared to achieve was massive destruction and a stalemate. While the United States could hold on militarily, what was it accomplishing in the process? This question changed the nature of the discussion about the war inside the Johnson administration, energized the antiwar movement, enlarged the credibility gap, and brought to the fore the economic crisis the war was creating in the United States. The interplay of the military battles and the growing political debate in the United States made Tet the pivotal moment of the war.

INTELLIGENCE FAILURE

The Tet Offensive represented, in the words of National Security Council (NSC) staff member William Jorden, "the worst intelligence failure of the war."[1] Yet it should not have been a surprise at all. In public statements, North Vietnamese officials had indicated that an important battle was approaching, while numerous captured documents and prisoner interrogations spoke of a major winter–spring military campaign being planned. In addition, intelligence reports noted new buildups of enemy forces in the South, and an increasing number of coordinated attacks on American bases indicated an upcoming offensive and a change in strategy from the guerrilla war tactics used up to that point.

Intelligence papers prepared in Saigon in December 1967 concluded that the "recent upsurge in Communist military activity" represented a "new *tactical* departure" following a strategy set out by North Vietnamese commander Vo Nguyen Giap and others in articles earlier in the year. The upcoming winter–spring campaign, they reported, was seen by the National Liberation Front (NLF)/North Vietnamese Army (NVA) "as the 'decisive' phase of the war" and as a "crucial period where basic decisions concerning the future of the war must be made." Their plan was to launch "an all-out offensive . . . designed to gain decisive victory." The offensive, these reports concluded, was designed "to bring about a fundamental change in the balance of forces in South Vietnam" that would lead to "the withdrawal of American forces from South Vietnam and the establishment of a so-called 'coalition government' which will, in effect, be under VC/NVN control." While no definite date for victory was mentioned, the captured documents "strongly implied that it will be some time in 1968." In sum, "the war is probably nearing a turning point and that the outcome of the 1967–68 winter-spring campaign will in all likelihood determine the future direction of the war."[2]

Based on this material, the American Embassy issued a press release in early January that stated that "subordinate level Communist party activists of the National Liberation Front forces are being told that the final phase of the revolutionary war in South Viet-Nam is at hand." In particular, it pointed to a document captured on November 19, 1967 that proclaimed: "Central Headquarters concludes that the time has come for a direct revolution and that the opportunity for a general offensive and general uprising is within reach." It further noted that the plans called for attacks "upon the major towns and cities, including Saigon."[3]

At the same time as this evidence was being discovered and circulated, there were officials in both the State Department and the Central Intelligence Agency (CIA) that questioned the optimistic projections of their superiors concerning the progress that had been made in Vietnam. Their analysis portrayed an enemy that was much stronger than Military Assistance Command, Vietnam (MACV) or Ambassador Ellsworth Bunker were reporting and able to carry out a major offensive. According to Assistant Undersecretary of State Nicholas Katzenbach, there was a consensus among the "working level experts" on Vietnam that in a year "the enemy will still be very much with us, that it will remain difficult to produce dramatic and convincing evidence of a victory in the near future."[4] This stemmed from their conviction that when one included irregular, local self-defense forces, which General Westmoreland and the embassy did not, the NLF had greater numbers than reported. Moreover, Hanoi had "effectively adapted its tactics to cope with US military pressures." According to the CIA, "the struggle between allied forces and Communist regular units is beginning to go better from Hanoi's viewpoint, than it has for some time, despite heavy casualties and a steady erosion of Communist capabilities." The NLF and NVA "have managed to offset the advantage gained when US combat forces were introduced by a combination of continued heavy infiltration and timely shifts in strategy and tactics." In Hanoi's calculus of the war, "the price of victories to the US counts more than the cost of defeats to the Communists."[5]

The CIA cautioned that the apparent change in strategy by Hanoi was not "necessarily a last-ditch desperation gamble" or proof "that the Communists are on the verge of defeat."[6] Yet that is exactly how Westmoreland and other senior officials in Saigon saw the situation, and they dismissed the evidence at hand because it did not conform to their own assumptions and optimism about the progress being made in the war. To senior American officials, an offensive was beyond the capacity of the enemy to carry out and, therefore, the plans they uncovered could not be serious. It was merely propaganda designed to distract their own troops from the hopeless nature of their plight.

Rostow had Robert Ginsburgh, an Air Force Colonel assigned to the NSC, prepare a critique of the CIA's analysis for President Johnson because he believed that the "CIA is leaning against an excessive optimism that does not exist." Ginsburgh began by declaring that he "found it difficult to believe that the CIA document is talking about the same war we are." There was "no basis," he insisted, for the interpretation that the war was going better from Hanoi's vantage point. The enemy's tactics, he insisted, had not stopped progress in pacification or the attrition of NLF forces, and "they have been more costly for the enemy than for the allies despite the advantages of terrain, shorter supply lines, and close sanctuaries" they possessed.[7]

The embassy in Saigon, too, continued to report that the enemy's position in South Vietnam was steadily deteriorating and that the NLF had "shown no signs of being able to reverse this trend." Thus, even while reporting on the apparent NLF/NVA plans for an offensive, the embassy rejected the idea because it was "far beyond their capability to accomplish," and it doubted that Hanoi "expects to be able to achieve all that they have promised their troops." The only explanation was that it was a go-for-broke promise to the troops because "at current rates of attrition the present scale of the conflict cannot be continued for much longer."[8] Indeed, the captured documents were portrayed as "ambiguous," could not be taken as "conclusive evidence that such an order has been given," and probably represented propaganda "designed to inspire the fighting troops." Reflecting on how the optimism of the time kept them from believing the evidence at hand, one intelligence officer later stated that "if we'd gotten the whole battle plan, it wouldn't have been believed. It wouldn't have been credible to us."[9]

Senior American officials in Saigon did agree that the war was reaching a crucial phase, and they expected an enemy attack. It would come, they thought, against the American base at Khe Sanh and not the cities. Located in the northwest corner of South Vietnam, twelve miles from the Laotian border and fourteen miles from the Demilitarized Zone (DMZ), Khe Sanh was a critical base for protecting the northern provinces of South Vietnam and cutting off infiltration of troops to the South. Since early January, Giap was moving NVA divisions into the hills around the base, creating the impression that the goal was another victory similar to the defeat of the French at Dienbienphu in 1954. Indeed, a North Vietnamese defector told American officers that Khe Sanh was supposed to be another Dienbienphu. By the time the siege began on January 20, there were nearly 40,000 North Vietnamese troops surrounding the base.

The similarities between Dienbienphu and Khe Sanh were readily apparent. Both bases were isolated, surrounded by mountains that gave protection to the attacking forces, and cut off on the ground from supplies. Given this, aerial photographs of Dienbienphu were sent from Washington to Saigon where Westmoreland had his staff study the battle of Dienbienphu to see what could be learned about Giap's strategy and how it might help in the defense of Khe Sanh.[10] President Johnson had a terrain map of Khe Sanh built and placed in the situation room at the White House so he could

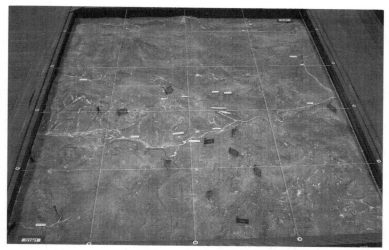

Photograph of the map of Khe Sanh used by President Johnson.

follow the battle. Johnson declared, "I don't want any damn Dienbienphu," and ordered the Joint Chiefs of Staff to pledge that Khe Sanh would not be lost.[11] The president told congressional leaders that he "almost had to have [the Joint Chiefs] signed up in blood, because if my poll goes where it has gone with all the victories, imagine what it would do if we had a major defeat." Westmoreland and the Joint Chiefs of Staff assured the president that they would defend the base, and reinforcements were sent to augment the troops already there, bringing the total to 6,000 marines. Their orders were to defend the base at all costs.[12]

The decision to launch the Tet Offensive was made in Hanoi in July 1967. The North knew it was locked in a costly stalemate on the battlefield and that it lacked the military capacity to defeat U.S. forces in the field. It also believed, however, that the United States could not endlessly escalate or fight forever. Hanoi, therefore, had to demonstrate to Washington that it would not be defeated and could increase the costs of the fighting for the United States beyond what it was willing to pay. For the next six months, troops and supplies were moved into place to prepare for what the Lao Dong Party (Communist Party) leaders called the General Offensive and General Uprising. As General Vo Nguyen Giap noted, the strategy of the Tet Offensive was "never purely military." It was an integrated military, political, and diplomatic strategy designed to take advantage of what the North saw as the two main weaknesses of their adversaries, the weakness of the Saigon government and public opposition to the war in the United States.

The General Offensive, therefore, had multiple goals. The most ambitious was that military victories would lead to a general uprising organized by NLF cadres that would bring about the collapse of the regime of President Nguyen Van Thieu and the creation of a coalition government. Under these conditions, the United States would be forced to leave. Short of these achievements, and aware that 1968 was an election year, a nationwide offensive would disprove the American claims of progress, demonstrate the war was a stalemate, and bring new pressure on Washington to change its course, end the U.S. escalation of the fighting, and force negotiations on their terms. Finally, it sought to bring the war to the urban population for the first time and in the process relieve the pressure on the countryside and the NLF strongholds that had suffered the brunt of American firepower and troops.[13]

The fall attacks in the provinces of Quang Tri and Thua Thien, just below the DMZ, and the siege at Khe Sanh were designed as a diversion to both conceal the movements of troops and supplies around the cities and pull American forces into the countryside. Westmoreland responded by moving forces out toward the borders of South Vietnam to meet enemy attacks near their bases and sanctuaries and begin what he saw as the final phase of the fighting. In response to increased enemy movements around populated areas, Lieutenant General Frederick Weyand convinced Westmoreland in mid-January to redeploy some American forces back from the border areas to the cities.[14] This movement better positioned the troops to respond to the attacks on Tet, and certainly prevented the NLF from gaining control of numerous targets, but Weyand's caution did not diminish the surprise.

THE YEAR OF THE MONKEY

The National Liberation Front struck in the early morning hours of the first day of the Tet cease-fire, shattering the quiet with their attacks throughout South Vietnam. In Saigon, sappers blew a hole in the wall of the U.S. Embassy compound and entered its grounds while other units attacked the South Vietnamese presidential palace, the national radio station, Tan Son Nhut airport, and numerous strategic locations throughout the capital. The scenario was the same in other cities as NLF forces coordinated their attacks on key government and military installations, including twenty-four airfields, seized control of the old imperial capital of Hue, and appeared to be everywhere at once. The Year of the Monkey on the Vietnamese calendar was to be the decisive one in the war.

The immediate reaction of American officials was to fit the attacks into their previously conceived notions of the enemy's plans. Thus, they saw the strikes against the cities as a diversionary tactic from the main objective, the overrunning of Khe Sanh, a test of American will, and a last-gasp effort to gain victory. Westmoreland reported that his assessment of the enemy strategy was "that this was a major, go-for-broke offensive" designed to distract MACV from the main effort around Khe Sanh, and that "the enemy would shortly run out of steam."[15] Robert McNamara told the Cabinet on January 31 that "we predicted this push in I Corps," and that this new offensive "appears to be a maximum effort to divert us away from Khe Sanh to the 24 airfields and other targets." It was bound to fail as "we have the mobility and firepower to handle it," and it will be "a big defeat for North Vietnam."[16] Similarly, the chairman of the Joint Chiefs of Staff, General Earle Wheeler, reported the same day that the attacks "are diversionary efforts, while the enemy prepares for his major attack . . . in the Que Son [Khe Sanh] area, we think. His targeting of airfields are designed to hinder friendly air support." The objectives of the attacks were to "draw our forces away from the reinforcements which General Westmoreland has sent to the north" to protect Khe Sanh while at the same time seeking "to shake the confidence of the Vietnamese people in the ability of the government to provide security." All of this advice led Johnson to inform congressional leaders that the attacks were a prelude to the main goal, "a massive attack in Quang Tri" against the base at Khe Sanh. "The enemy is now poised for this phase, General Westmoreland says, which he considers his decisive campaign."[17]

The CIA concurred that the series of coordinated enemy attacks were preparations "to a major assault in the Khe Sanh area" and that they could not succeed militarily. It disagreed, however, concerning the ultimate goals of the Tet Offensive, seeing it as "designed for maximum psychological impact and to demonstrate the Communists' continued power despite the presence of US forces." The intelligence

Map of the Tet Offensive.

agency also questioned the notion that this was a final desperate bid by a defeated adversary, continuing to see evidence of enemy strength, "improved firepower, flexibility of tactics, and a considerable degree of resiliency. The current offensive is probably," it concluded, "intended to convey the impression that despite VC problems and despite half a million US troops, the Communists are still powerful and capable of waging war."[18]

The seizure of a navy intelligence ship, the U.S.S. *Pueblo*, by North Korea on January 23 added to the crisis atmosphere in Washington. The administration believed from the first day that the taking of the ship was a coordinated action between the North Koreans and North Vietnamese to distract U.S. attention from Vietnam and put added pressure on U.S. resources. President Johnson believed it was designed to create another war scare in the United States, and that it "all ties in . . . to one large determined offensive of theirs [communists] that's calculated to try to put them back in the ball game." The president told the cabinet that when you "look at Pueblo, Khe Sanh, Saigon, and you can see them all as part of the Communist effort to defeat us out there." The military and CIA agreed with this assessment. General Taylor believed that the "Pueblo incident is linked to South Vietnam. It is an attempt to divert our attention, to create problems for us here at home in the United States." Richard Helms concurred, stating that it appeared "like collusion between the North Koreans and the Soviets" in support of North Vietnam.[19]

Johnson wrote Rusk and McNamara that "it appears to be the judgment of our enemies that we are sufficiently weak and uncertain at home, sufficiently stretched in our military dispositions abroad, and sufficiently anxious to end the war in Viet Nam so that we are likely to accept, if not defeat, at least some degree of humiliation." This accounted for the timing of the seizure of the *Pueblo* and the "attacks on the cities and towns and airfields in South Viet Nam." It was critical, he informed them, that American resolve not be found wanting and that "one way or another in the days ahead, we have to rally our country so that the enemy comes to believe" that the United States will not back down.[20]

In order to help rally support, the White House cabled Ambassador Bunker and General Westmoreland on January 31 a request that they appear in front of the press, despite the pressures they were under in the midst of the attacks, in order to help shape the public interpretation of the events. "We are facing, in these next few days," Press Secretary George Christian wrote, "a critical phase in the American public's understanding and confidence toward our effort in Vietnam." While the administration was confident that the American military would succeed, "it is imperative that the public here at home be given the understanding which supports this outlook. There is no more effective way in which this can be accomplished than by personal appearances by each of you with the press." Specifically, "nothing can more dramatically counter scenes of VC destructiveness than the confident professionalism of our commanding general. Similarly, the dire prognostications of our commentators can best be put into perspective by the shared experience and wisdom of our ambassador." It was the president's belief "that now is the time for you to step forward and give your fellow citizens a full and effective presentation of our position. If you do, they cannot help but respond in confidence and unity to the challenges of the moment."[21]

Accordingly, Westmoreland met with reporters on the street outside the U.S. Embassy compound the next day. When asked what he thought the purpose of the attacks was, the general responded that the "enemy, very deceitfully, has taken advantage of the Tet truce in order to create maximum consternation within South Vietnam. . . . In my opinion, this is diversionary to his main effort which he had planned to take place in Quang Tri province from Laos to Khe Sanh and across the Demilitarized Zone." Westmoreland set out his view that the Tet Offensive was a last-gasp effort by the enemy to avoid defeat and his confidence that American forces had the situation in hand. "The enemy," he concluded, had "exposed himself by this strategy and he has suffered great casualties."[22]

The president also appeared in public to reassure the nation and rally support for the war. International communism, Johnson stated, was testing the will of the United States, but the country would not falter. Reminding the country of the main reasons for the war, he declared on February 1 that "we are fighting now—as we fought 25 years ago—to prevent any further expansion of totalitarian coercion over the souls of men."[23] The next day Johnson held a press conference where he downplayed the element of surprise and presented the battles as an American victory. He began by stating that the administration knew several months in advance "that the Communists planned a massive winter-spring offensive." Its first objective "was to overthrow the constitutional government in Saigon and to create a situation in which we and the Vietnamese would be willing to accept the Communist–dominated coalition government." "The biggest fact," the president continued, was that the enemy was being defeated both politically and militarily. "The stated purposes of the general uprising have failed. Communist leaders counted on popular support in the cities for their efforts. They found little or none." Moreover, all agreed that "as a military movement it has been a failure" as well. The enemy had already lost over 10,000 killed while the United States had only lost 249 men. The president compared the offensive to an urban riot, noting that the NLF had disrupted the country, but it was not a significant military campaign and would not lead to any change in American strategy.[24]

The second objective, Johnson claimed, was "a psychological victory. We have to realize that in moments of tenseness and trial . . . that there will be a great effort to exploit that and let that substitute for military victory they have not achieved." In this area, Johnson was confident that the offensive would fail as well. When asked, in light of the attacks on the cities, if the United States was still winning the war, the president stated that he saw "nothing in the developments" of the past few days "that would indicate that the

Secretary of Defense Robert McNamara briefing congressional leaders January 30, 1968.

evaluation that I have had of this situation" should be changed. While he claimed he was "not a great strategist and tactician," he could count. Given the enormous differences in casualties, he stated that it "does not look like a Communist victory." Rather, it was a last ditch effort and that "it looks like somebody has paid a very dear price for the temporary encouragement that some of our enemies had."[25]

American and allied forces had responded quickly to the attacks, taking back strategic points in the first days of the fighting and systematically subduing enemy soldiers in every city. In the process, American officials praised the performance of the Saigon government and ARVN during the fighting and claimed that the lack of an uprising indicated the Thieu government had the support of the people. Still the fighting raged in Saigon, Dalat, and other cities for three weeks before they were secured, and in Hue the combined NLF/NVA force was not dislodged until the end of February when they were finally driven from the Citadel. Even when they were repulsed, enemy forces continued to fight just outside major population centers such as Saigon and Danang to maintain the pressure on American forces and the Saigon government. In the process, enemy casualties were staggering, around 58,000 by the end of March, leading American commanders to continue to claim a significant victory. The full significance of Tet, however, cannot be measured in just these terms.

WHAT THE HELL IS GOING ON?

The size and breadth of the attack were stunning enough, but the images coming out of South Vietnam in the early days added to the shock and impact of the offensive. Television reports showed the fighting on the embassy grounds, chaos in the streets of Saigon, the assassination of an NLF prisoner by a South Vietnamese general on a Saigon street, and pitched battles in other cities such as Hue, while the Associated Press reported an American officer in the village of Ben Tre stating that "we had to destroy it in order to save it."[26] Walter Cronkite, the well-respected and trusted CBS News anchor, represented the views of many Americans when he declared upon receiving the first reports on the Tet Offensive: "What the hell is going on? I thought we were winning the war!"[27]

The destruction caused by the fighting was horrific. Large parts of Saigon and other cities lay in rubble and ruin. In Hue, almost 10,000 of its 17,000 houses were destroyed and refugees clogged all of the major roads and over-whelmed the resources of the government. As General Palmer described the carnage in Hue, after the fighting "the beautiful city . . . was a shattered, stinking hulk, its streets choked with rubble and rotting bodies."[28] Later, on the out-skirts of the city, more evidence of the costs of the bitter fighting was discovered in a massive grave of 2,800 people who were killed by the revolutionary forces while they con-trolled the city.

Palmer's portrayal of Hue could be applied to dozens of other cities as well. Despite the Johnson administration's best efforts, it did not look much like victory to many peo-ple. Rather, as critics charged, the Tet Offensive contradicted all of the optimistic claims made the previous fall. The NLF/NVA had replaced their losses and were not losing a war of attrition. The other side still had enormous strength and vitality and could launch an offensive. The enemy was not defeated and the United States did not have control over the situation. The fact that intense fighting continued into

March and beyond after all of the cities were cleared indicated that it was not a last gasp and that the fighting would continue with no apparent end in sight. In short, the United States was not winning.

The administration's immediate worries about public opinion belied its victory declarations and showed that it was more concerned about the attacks than its public statements indicated. In a memorandum on February 3 for Rostow, William Jorden set out the range of problems the Tet Offensive exposed. He acknowledged "that the North Vietnamese and VC paid a heavy price for this adventure," but doubted "that either the VC or the general Vietnamese population are as impressed as we are by these losses." Rather, the attacks "have severely shaken confidence in the Government's ability to provide security to its people." It also raised doubts about the claims of pacification and control made by the United States. "If the VC and North Vietnamese can move probably 30,000 men into place for attacks in all part of the country without detection" then something was wrong with the intelligence and information available to Saigon. In addition to the troops, "thousands of Vietnamese must have been aware of movements through or near their villages, and of unusual activity in their neighborhoods in the cities." Yet no one reported these. The result was that "we didn't have one single attack thoroughly anticipated." All this "cast serious doubt on any future statements that people in Viet-Nam's urban centers are 'under Government control' or 'free from VC threat.' They clearly are not."[29]

Clark Clifford recalled that a "tense atmosphere" pervaded the White House in early February. Johnson was "gravely concerned about the likelihood of another VC/NVA offensive," and "there was much deliberation about the prospects of ARVN collapsing and the potential instability of the SVN government." These fears were aggravated by the potential for crises in other parts of the world and mounting domestic problems.[30] Presidential speech writer Harry McPherson later noted that February "was really the most dismaying month I ever remember in the White House."[31]

While continuing to report a military victory, Westmoreland acknowledged that "the attacks undoubtedly came as a surprise to the people [of Saigon] and gave the enemy an initial psychological edge" as the "size and violence of the VC attacks and the discipline and dedication of their forces were impressive, as was their ability to infiltrate." Given this, it was necessary to "accept the fact that the enemy has dealt the [Government of South Vietnam] a severe blow. He has brought the war to the towns and cities and has inflicted damage and casualties on the population."[32] Destruction was everywhere, "distribution of the necessities of life has been interrupted . . . and the economy has been disrupted." This placed tremendous strains on the Saigon government "to restore stability and to aid the people who have suffered" that it was not well prepared to meet.

This point was well understood in Washington. President Johnson wired Ambassador Bunker on February 3 that it was "time to let Thieu know how important it is that he . . . move rapidly on some of the deeper problems facing the Vietnamese government." It was clear that the "coordinated NVA/VC attacks and the enemy's extensive propaganda campaign have had a strongly negative effect on both Vietnamese and American opinion." These included the need for "strengthening ARVN" by getting better officers in command, combating rampant corruption, and improving intelligence. "It is a disgrace," Johnson wrote, "that the VC can mount dozens of attacks all over the country and his

Government doesn't know a thing about it in advance." The crisis demanded leadership from Thieu, not his usual "cautious approach to problems."[33]

Concerns were also arising about the military side of the conflict. As late as February 9, Westmoreland was still portraying the enemy offensive as a desperate action, stemming from its weakness and inability to continue a protracted conflict "in view of the success of our ground and air actions against his forces" and anticipating what he continued to believe was the main goal, the attack "against Khe Sanh with the objective of establishing military control over the two northern provinces." Yet in a contradiction to claims that American forces had decimated the enemy on the battlefield, America's commanding general acknowledged that at present "an enemy threat of major proportions" still existed, and that the ARVN was significantly weakened and would take "at least six months" to restore its strength. These realities led Westmoreland to request more troops. "Needless to say," Westmoreland wrote Wheeler, "I would welcome reinforcements at any time they can be made available" to offset losses, counter enemy actions and reinforcements, and "go on the offensive as soon as his attack is spent."[34]

That same day, General Wheeler provided President Johnson a bleak progress report based on Westmoreland's message and made the case for more troops. "There is a question," Wheeler stated, "whether the ARVN can stand up after 12 days of heavy fighting if another series of heavy attacks occur." Westmoreland needed reinforcements "to prevent the ARVN from falling apart" and to provide a reserve to respond to further enemy attacks. McNamara noted that the specific request would mean 40,000 more men on top of the 500,000 already in Vietnam. This request raised disturbing and difficult questions for the president. Johnson

Secretary of State Dean Rusk.

noted that since the attacks he had asked if Westmoreland had all he needed and was it sufficient to handle the situation, and each time the answer to both questions was yes. "Tell me," he said to Wheeler, "what has happened to change the situation between then and now." Wheeler responded that they had new intelligence that indicated the enemy had 15,000 more men than they thought, and that the ratio of U.S. troops to enemy troops was 1.4 to 1 and not 1.7 to 1 as believed in December. Johnson was incredulous at what he heard. "What you are saying is this," the president declared. "Since last week we have information we did not know about earlier. This is the addition of 15,000 North Vietnamese in the northern part of the country. Because of that, do we need 15 U.S. battalions?"[35]

The discussion then turned to Khe Sanh, where the Joint Chiefs could give holding the base no more than a

50–50 chance. McNamara noted that the reality was that the enemy had been hurt but still has "the ability to re-strike." This led Clifford to point out the "very strange contradiction in what we are saying and doing." Publicly, the secretary of defense-designate noted, "we are saying that we have known of this build up" and that the offensive did not create an uprising, cost the enemy dearly in casualties, and was an American victory. "Now our reaction to all of that is to say that the situation is more dangerous today than it was before all of this," that we need more troops and equipment, and "that we need to call up the reserves." Clifford wanted to know "how we explain saying on one hand the enemy did not take a victory and yet we are in need of many more troops and possibly an emergency call up." Johnson responded by stating the "only explanation I see" is that the enemy had changed its strategy and put "all of their stack in now," meaning he had "to be prepared for all that we might face." Rusk ended the meeting with a pregnant question that received no answer. "In the past, we have said the problem really was finding the enemy. Now the enemy has come to us. I am sure many will ask why we aren't doing better under these circumstances, now that we know where they are."[36]

The discussion of more troops would preoccupy the administration for the next three weeks. On February 12, Westmoreland submitted "a firm request for additional troops." In an unintentional admission that previous reports of progress were inaccurate, the general noted that while he did not fear defeat if the request was denied, he could not "fully grasp the initiative from the recently reinforced enemy without them." Conversely, he said that "a set back is fully possible if I am not reinforced" and that it was "likely that we will lose ground in other areas" if an attack comes at Khe Sanh and he needed to shift additional troops there to hold the base. It remained, according to Westmoreland, the greatest threat, and he was determined to defend the base or else the enemy would threaten all of the northern provinces. Moreover, "the psychological impact of a withdrawal . . . after the recent VC splurge in the cities . . . would be a heavy blow to the confidence of the people and government of SVN, and possibly a large segment of the American public."[37]

Westmoreland's latest cable created confusion in the White House. In a meeting of the president with his senior foreign policy advisors, all agreed that they should send the troops Westmoreland requested. But no one thought this answered all their questions or solved the problems created by the Tet Offensive. Everyone recognized that the communist forces were stronger than they previously believed. McNamara thought that Westmoreland wanted the extra battalions "in order to avoid defeat at Khesanh." Clifford continued to raise the question of what had changed, why Westmoreland "says in his cable that he cannot hold without reinforcements," and why the "telegram has a much greater sense of urgency in it?" Why not, Clifford wanted to know, move forces from other areas of the country rather than send additional troops? Wheeler's responses indicated the difficulties the military faced as forces were stretched thin throughout the nation to defend the cities and main roads. Westmoreland could not "take more forces from the South without risk." His previous troop requests were too conservative and he now "finds that his campaign plan has been pre-empted by enemy action." The president also noted that Westmoreland went from saying "he could use troops one day" to making "an urgent request for them" a few days later. Johnson told his advisors that he was "scared about Khesanh" and that he could not endure many losses. "I have a mighty big stake in this. I am more unsure every day." Still, "if the Vietnamese aren't able to carry the load we will have to do it rather than let them all get defeated. I think Westmoreland is confronted with a defeat or a victory."[38]

The much-touted victory was looking more tenuous all the time as other reports undercut the optimistic appraisals of Westmoreland and Bunker. The State Department's study of the countryside in the wake of Tet showed that "as a result of their urban offensive the Viet Cong have expanded their control in South Vietnam's rural areas and have made pacification virtually inoperative." As U.S. and ARVN forces were pulled back to defend the cities, they left a vacuum in the countryside that the NLF has filled. It now appeared that this move in the rural areas "was an integral part of the Communist plan" to take full advantage of the withdrawal of allied troops to the cities. "The guerrillas were able to move into the vacuum and establish general control over much of the rural area" in all parts of the country, "overrunning and harassing outposts, invading previously secure hamlets, conducting propaganda, organizing, recruiting, interdicting roads . . . establishing hamlet administrations, and obtaining food and other supplies." In the Mekong Delta, the NLF was "stronger now than they ever were," while in the other regions "the countryside belongs to the VC."[39]

With rural security collapsing, "the pacification program now appears to be almost inoperative" as the NLF took over villages and hamlets previously declared safe. Optimistic estimates were that "pacification will take 18 months to reach the same stage of development that existed six months ago." That effort faced numerous problems, most notably that "the rural population has seen the VC mount a large scale far-ranging offensive throughout the country, one that succeeded in penetrating many hitherto inviolate urban areas." This achievement and the destruction brought about by the fighting "appear to have complicated further the task of winning allegiance." One province official reported that "years of hard work . . . was destroyed in 30 minutes of military action, not to mention the propaganda value such destruction gives to the VC," while another informed Saigon that the pacification program in his province "is at a halt" and would be for a long time as the South Vietnamese government focused on the urban problems and refugees. The State Department's intelligence memorandum concluded that the "VC urban offensive has dealt a heavy blow to the GVN presence in the countryside and has set back pacification significantly."[40]

The CIA reported at the end of February that although the toll on communist forces was high, the infiltration of new troops continued and "a significant part of the guerrilla and Main forces could still be committed" to the fighting. "And, at present, the Communists enjoy fuller access to the rural areas, where they are recruiting heavily" allowing them to "recoup their recent losses, though at some sacrifice in quality." Thus, "the Communists probably will maintain their offensive for the next several months and be prepared to accept the high losses this entails." Nor was this an end to the war-now strategy. Rather, the struggle would continue "should the present phase fail to produce a decisive result." On the other side, the position of the Saigon government "has been weakened. Its prestige has suffered from the shock of the Tet offensive; its control over the countryside has been greatly reduced." While there was no general uprising, "neither was there a rallying to the government side." On balance, the CIA believed the odds were "no better than even" that Saigon "will emerge from the present phase without being still further weakened."[41]

As the fighting continued, raising new doubts and questions in the American public, Johnson sought to keep up the nation's morale and resolve to fight. On the weekend of February 17–18, the president visited the reinforcement troops that were departing for Vietnam. He spoke confidently of the duty and obligation to defend freedom from aggression and of the defeat of the enemy's offensive in Vietnam. "After 2½ years in which he has seen his grip on the people weaken, he has finally decided to try to win now— this year. His aim is to shake the Government of South Vietnam to its foundations, to shake the confidence of the South Vietnamese people, to destroy the will of your people—the American people—to see this struggle through." In this attempt "he failed." It was a decisive time, Johnson declared, with all the world watching the brave American soldiers defending Khe Sanh. "We do not doubt the outcome." He was sure that the "enemy's tide will be broken."[42]

With reports from Saigon filled with inconsistencies, if not outright contradictions, growing doubts about the veracity of Westmoreland's claims of victory, and numerous questions and disagreements within the administration about the actual state of the war, the decision was made to send General Wheeler to Saigon to examine the situation and provide a firsthand evaluation to the president. Wheeler spent three days there, February 23–25, meeting with Westmoreland and other American officials. En route home to Washington, he told reporters that there would be "no early end to this war" and that the American public "must expect hard fighting to continue."[43] In his report to Johnson on February 27, the chairman of the Joint Chiefs of Staff presented a sobering picture of the fighting along with a shocking request for over 200,000 more troops. "There is no doubt," he began, "that the enemy launched a major powerful nation-wide assault against the Government of South Vietnam" and that "this offensive has by no means run its course." All of the American commanders in the four corps areas of Vietnam "agree that [the] initial attack nearly succeeded in a dozen places and the margin of victory—in some places survival—was very very small indeed."[44] It was only the quick reactions of American forces that prevented these defeats. "In short, it was a very near thing."[45] Army Chief of Staff General Harold K. Johnson was less circumspect, stating, "we suffered a loss, there can be no doubt about it."[46]

Nor was the worst necessarily over. "The scope and severity of his attacks and the extent of his reinforcements are presenting us with serious and immediate problems" with "heavy fighting ahead." While the enemy was hurt during the attacks and had suffered heavy losses, it was clear that the offensive would continue and that "he has the capability to do so." He controlled the countryside where in most areas "the pacification program has been brought to a halt." Conversely, "there is some question as to whether the South Vietnamese Armed Forces have the stamina to withstand the pressure of a prolonged enemy offensive." American troops were stretched to the limit because they had to support ARVN forces as well as conduct their own operations. "Commanders are unanimous in the view that the VC would have achieved a number of significant local successes at the outset, except for timely reinforcement by US forces." Therefore, "at the very time General Westmoreland is redeploying and otherwise preparing to meet major thrusts by large NVA forces, he is forced to pick up part of the tab from ARVN." This left him with no theatre reserve, and "if the enemy synchronizes his expected major attacks with increased pressure throughout the country, General Westmoreland's margin will be paper thin."[47] It was the judgment of all American officials in Saigon that the NLF and NVA have "the will and the capability to continue," that their "determination appears to be unshaken" despite the casualties inflicted on them, and that "the enemy is operating with relative freedom in the countryside" and "recruiting heavily." That meant "his recovery is likely to be rapid."[48] In summary, Wheeler found that "the VC/NVA forces took the initiative and still hold it."[49]

Facing this situation, one that Wheeler characterized as "fraught with opportunities as well as dangers," the chairman requested an increased force of 206,000 men to provide Westmoreland "a theatre reserve and an offensive capacity which he does not now have."[50] This proposal, Clifford recalled, "simply astonished Washington" and shaped "the course of the war and American politics" after it.[51] They were no longer discussing a victory, as MACV was claiming in public, but holding on without any further setbacks. The damage was more extensive than anyone had thought, and dangers remained. This new reality would necessitate a calling up of the reserves, extending tours of duty up to six months, and increasing the number of draftees. All of this, if approved, would fundamentally change the nature of the war both in Vietnam and at home.

STALEMATE AND CRISES

The impact of the Tet Offensive was being felt outside of the corridors of power in Washington, DC, as well. Those who had already thought the war was a mistake found further convincing evidence while others who had questions but continued to back the administration, and were persuaded by its case in the fall of 1967, or had fully supported the war, now had reason to doubt the statements from American officials and reevaluate their views as the credibility gap widened. Tet dominated the news coverage on television, newspapers, and magazines as people followed the fighting in Saigon, Hue, and Khe Sanh to name only the most prominent stories, and saw the destruction and dislocation that was occurring throughout South Vietnam. The story was so significant that CBS anchorman Walter Cronkite went to Vietnam on February 11 for two weeks to report on the war. He met with American and South Vietnamese officials, toured the country, and reported from ongoing battles in Hue and other places. In his first report from Saigon, Cronkite told his audience that "first and simplest, the Viet Cong suffered a military defeat."[52] On his last day in Vietnam he interviewed an optimistic Ambassador Bunker who provided assurances that the United States had achieved a decisive military victory and that the enemy failed to accomplish any of their objectives.[53]

Upon his return to New York, Cronkite hosted a news special on the Vietnam War, the single most important news event on the offensive. At the end he provided his analysis of the war as a stalemate. He asked, "who won and who lost in the great Tet offensive against the cities?" Neither side, Cronkite concluded. He doubted American forces could be defeated, but "we have been too often disappointed by the optimism of the American leaders, both in Vietnam and Washington, to have faith any longer in the silver linings they find in the darkest clouds."[54] His concluding words, which Press Secretary George Christian later noted produced "shock waves [that] rolled through the government," indicated to Johnson that mainstream American society was no longer supportive of the war.[55] "To say that we are closer to victory today," Cronkite opined,

> is to believe, in the face of the evidence, the optimists who have been wrong in the past. To suggest we are on the edge of defeat is to yield to unreasonable pessimism. To say that we are mired in stalemate seems the only realistic, yet unsatisfactory, conclusion. On the off chance that military and political analysts are right, in the next few months we must test the enemy's intentions, in case this is indeed his last gasp before negotiations. But it is increasingly clear to this reporter that the only rational way out then will be to negotiate, not as victors, but as an honorable people who lived up to their pledge to defend democracy, and did the best they could.[56]

Tet did not cause a dramatic shift in public opinion. Rather, polls indicated that the slight improvement of support for the war in the wake of the fall 1967 public relations campaign was ended by Tet and the trend of a steady decline of support for the war returned. By March, 49 percent thought the war was a mistake and only 41 percent did not. In addition, President Johnson's overall approval ratings dropped from 48 to 36 percent.[57] In the fall, 50 percent of the population thought the United States was making progress in Vietnam, and only 8 percent thought it was losing the war. In February, only 33 percent now believed the United States was making progress while 38 percent saw the war as a stalemate and 23 percent thought the United States was now losing.[58]

More troubling news was arriving on the economic front, where the costs of the Vietnam War continued to multiply for the Johnson administration. When Johnson sent the first American ground troops to Vietnam in 1965 the economy was at the height of the post–World War II economic boom and the president was assured by his advisors that the nation could afford both the increasing commitment in Vietnam and the Great Society, both guns and butter. The chairman of the Council of Economic Advisers, Gardner Ackley, informed Johnson in July 1965 that "*our economy has lots of room to absorb a defense step-up,*" because "our *productive capacity is growing by $25–30 billion a year . . .* making room for both more butter and, if needed, more guns." Indeed, if the costs followed McNamara's July 1965 projections for the war the increased expenditures "*could provide a significant stimulus to economic activity during the first half of next year.*" Ackley was "certainly not saying that a Vietnam crisis is just what the doctor ordered for the American economy. . . . But, on a coldly objective analysis, *the over-all effects are most likely to be favorable to our prosperity.*"[59]

This optimism reflected the confidence of the New Economics of the postwar years. Adopting Keynesian economic policies, economists such as Ackley believed that with the proper mix of fiscal and monetary policies, the government could so manage the economy that continuous economic growth could be sustained without significant inflation and low unemployment. When asked at a Senate hearing how long the nation could afford the war, McNamara replied: "I think forever." There were, the secretary of defense claimed, "many things, many prices we pay for the war in Vietnam, some heavy prices indeed, but in my opinion one of them is not strain on our economy."[60]

Yet escalation increased at a more rapid pace and to numbers higher than originally projected, and the cost of the war quickly outpaced the estimated projections and appropriations. By 1967, the war was costing over $2 billion a month and rising with no end in sight. Johnson was forced, in 1967, to ask for a tax surcharge to meet this rising bill and the growing federal deficit it was creating, over 25 billion dollars in 1968. Congress, however, refused to pass a tax bill in 1967. As Godfrey Hodgson has noted, "the *economy* could afford both guns and butter. The snag was that the federal *budget* could not, unless it transferred resources from the private sector . . . without running a deficit," which given full employment would mean inflation.[61] And that is exactly what happened. For the first five years of the 1960s, the Consumer Price Index (CPI) rose only 1.2 percent, less than .25 percent a year, while the economy grew at record rates. By 1966, however, the CPI went up 3.4 percent, and two years later the rate stood at 4.7 percent.[62] The reappearance of inflation, along with the social unrest caused by the war, added to the uneasiness of the American public with the war. If this was not bad enough, the deficit and inflation helped bring about a gold crisis in the winter of 1967–1968 that threatened to create an international trade crisis and send the economy into a recession.

Since the 1944 Bretton Woods conference, the United States had served as the world's banker, with the value of the U.S. dollar set at $35 to an ounce of gold. Because of this, international trade was mainly carried out in dollars, and foreign central banks were willing to hold onto dollars because they held their purchasing power, earned interest, and provided access to the capital markets in the United States, by far the world's largest. To support the conversion pledge, the United States held $12 billion in gold stock, representing 75 percent of the dollars held by other nations' central banks and nearly 40 percent of both official and private dollar holdings. The system was built on confidence in the U.S. economy. As Rostow told Johnson, "even with large reserves, the dollar can be shaken by a drop in confidence." If foreign holders of dollars feared a drop in its value, a devaluation, and a concomitant increase in the price of gold, they would turn in their dollars for gold. "Similarly," he continued, "an inflationary rise in our prices can make them shift out of dollars" due to the fear of the drop in the purchasing power of the dollar and "because they know inflation can lead to devaluation."[63]

In the last six weeks of 1967, the gold pool in London, that was established to meet all the international demands for gold at the conversion rate, lost $1.5 billion. This was caused by a combination of the devaluation of the British pound sterling, the growing American trade deficit, and the onset of inflation in the United States. As one report noted, "most observers believe that a strong U.S. balance of payments program would be a major factor in restoring confidence in the gold market." During the last quarter of 1967, the United States had a $7 billion balance of payments deficit. All of this threatened "an intolerable drain upon our and our partners' gold reserves."[64]

By January, the problem had become acute. Ackley informed Johnson that there was a *"risk* of a critical deterioration of the world economic situation—one that could even lead to a world depression if prompt action were not taken to reverse it."[65] The crisis continued to grow, with losses by March totaling nearly $2 billion of gold leaving the United States, since the beginning of the year, to meet the demand. Rostow warned the president in February that the "situation could turn into a crisis of confidence and feed on itself—much like a run on a bank." It could result in "a serious contraction of international liquidity and pressure on all countries to adopt restrictive economic policies—at home and abroad—to preserve their gold holdings."[66] In response to the crisis, Johnson again asked Congress to pass a tax surcharge of 10 percent to finance the war, ease the deficit problems, and restore confidence in the U.S. economy. An informal meeting of leading New York bankers and Treasury officials concluded that "the tax bill is a must" for solving the problem, along with institutional reforms in how the gold pool operated.[67] When finally passed, the legislature cut $6 billion in spending on social programs as its price for a tax increase. As one scholar has noted, the tax hike and spending cuts meant "the promise of guns and butter was broken."[68]

On March 14, when, according to the National Security Council, "gold speculation reached panic proportions" after a one-day loss of $372 million and the anticipation of "losing perhaps $1 billion in gold tomorrow," the Treasury closed the gold market and held an emergency meeting that weekend in Washington with the central bankers from the gold pool countries to reform the system.[69] The agreements reached, the Council of Economic Advisers informed Johnson, were well received by governments and financiers, but they were only temporary measures to maintain the system until more permanent adjustments could be made, and were designed as "a means of providing *breathing space for the United States* to correct its balance of payments; and *futile unless we get the tax increase*, and bring our domestic house in order."[70]

Adding to Johnson's troubles that February was the presidential campaign of 1968 looming on the near horizon. In the fall of 1967, Senator Eugene McCarthy of Minnesota announced he would challenge Johnson in the primaries for the Democratic Party nomination as an anti-war candidate. At first, few gave the soft-spoken McCarthy any chance of gaining significant support, much less upsetting a sitting president and becoming the Democratic nominee. He was supported, however, by a dedicated faction of the party that sought to dump Johnson and use the election as a referendum on the war. Hundreds of young people volunteered to go to New Hampshire and canvass for his campaign, going "Clean for Gene" to rally support for their candidate and in doing so end the war.

The Tet Offensive provided an enormous boost to McCarthy's campaign as his criticisms of the war, and his candidacy, gained wide coverage and new supporters. McCarthy charged that the "Administration's reports of progress are the products of their own self-deception. . . . Their [the Communists'] attacks on the cities of South Vietnam show that we don't have the country under any kind of control and that we are in a much worse position than we were in two years ago." Prior to Tet, polls showed McCarthy with only single-digit support among Democratic voters. In February, that number climbed to 18 percent and was growing.[71] Johnson, who had not yet declared his candidacy, was now faced with a battle in the upcoming primaries, and the possibility that Robert Kennedy might join the race if McCarthy demonstrated that the president was politically vulnerable.

By the end of February, with the military asking for more troops, opposition to the war spreading, economic problems reaching troubling proportions, and a challenge in the primaries, Johnson faced a myriad of problems. Even though he would not officially take office for two more days, the president appointed Clifford on February 28 to chair a task force to study the troop request and make its recommendations to him by Monday, March 4. This was to be an "A to Z" reassessment of the American strategy in Vietnam.[72] The president wanted "alternatives examined and, if possible, agreed recommendations to emerge which reconcile the military, diplomatic, economic, Congressional, and public opinion problems involved" from an increase in American forces.[73]

The troop request would bring into focus all of the military, diplomatic, political, and economic issues raised by the Tet Offensive. As the Defense Department's internal history of Vietnam decisions, the *Pentagon Papers*, note, "a fork in the road had been reached" by the Johnson administration.[74] The military was asking that it change strategy from one of limited war with controlled costs to a complete commitment of American forces to Vietnam and a possible escalation of the conflict beyond Vietnam's borders. This would necessitate a greater sacrifice from the nation through a call-up of the reserves and going on wartime footing with additional economic sacrifices. Critics sought a reevaluation of American policy to acknowledge that the military and economic problems that confronted the nation demonstrated the untenable nature of the American effort no matter how many resources were poured into the war, and to use the crisis created by Tet to provide a way out of Vietnam. The examination of the questions, analysis of the issues, and debates produced by Clifford's task force would bring about a fundamental change in American policy.

NOTES

1. Jorden to Rostow, "Situation in Vietnam," February 3, 1968, NSF: CO Vietnam, Box 62, LBJL.

2. Rostow to Johnson, December 15, 1967, "Papers on Viet Cong Strategy"; "Overview of Viet Cong Strategy"; and "The Viet Cong/North Vietnamese Winter-Spring Campaign," December 8, 1967, NSF: Memos to the President: Rostow, Box 26, LBJL (emphasis in the original).

3. Don Oberdorfer, *TET!* (New York: Avon Books, 1971), 136.

4. Katzenbach to Rusk, November 1, 1967, Gibbons Papers, Box 32, LBJL.

5. On troop strength, see Marilyn Young, *The Vietnam Wars, 1945–1990* (New York: HarperCollins, 1991), 214, and Edward Moise, "Why Westmoreland Gave Up," *Pacific Affairs*, vol. 58, no. 4 (Winter 1985–86), 663–73; Intelligence Memorandum, "A Review of the Situation in Vietnam," December 8, 1967, Gibbons Papers, Box 33, LBJL.

6. Carver to Rostow, December 15, 1967, NSF: Memos to the President, Rostow, Box 26, LBJL.

7. Rostow to Johnson and Ginsburgh to Rostow, December 13, 1967, Gibbons Papers, Box 33, LBJL.

8. "Overview of Viet Cong Strategy," and "The Viet Cong/North Vietnamese Winter-Spring Campaign," December 8, 1967, NSF: Memos to the President: Rostow, Box 26, LBJL.

9. Oberdorfer, *TET!*, 136–39.

10. Oberdorfer, *TET!*, 126–27.

11. Video, "The Tet Offensive," *The Vietnam War with Walter Cronkite* (New York: CBS Video Library, 1985).

12. Congressional Leadership Briefing, January 31, 1968, Congressional Briefings on Vietnam, Box 1, LBJL.

13. "Directive on Forthcoming Offensive and Uprisings," November 1, 1967, in Steven Cohen, ed., *Vietnam: Anthology and Guide to A Television History* (New York: Knopf, 1983), 201–03; Ngo Vinh Long, "The Tet Offensive and Its Aftermath," *Indochina Newsletter*, Nos. 49, 50, 51.

14. Oberdorfer, *TET!*, 155–56.

15. General Westmoreland's History Notes, February 1, 1968, Gibbons Papers, Box 35, LBJL.

16. Cabinet Meeting, January 31, 1968, Cabinet Papers, Box 12, LBJL.

17. Congressional Leadership Briefing, January 31, 1968, Congressional Briefings on Vietnam, Box 1, LBJL.

18. Intelligence Memorandum, "The Communist Tet Offensive," January 31, 1968, NSF: CO Vietnam, Box 75, LBJL.

19. Notes on the President's Meeting with the National Security Council, January 24, 1968, Gibbons Papers, Box 34, LBJL; Congressional Leadership Briefing, January 31, 1968, Congressional Briefings on Vietnam, Box 1, LBJL; Cabinet Meeting, January 31, 1968, Cabinet Papers, Box 12, LBJL.

20. Johnson to Secretary of State, Secretary of Defense, and Director, Bureau of the Budget, January 31, 1968, Gibbons Papers, Box 34, LBJL.

21. Christian to Bunker and Westmoreland, January 31, 1968, NSF: CO Vietnam, Box 100, LBJL.

22. Video, "The Tet Offensive," *The Vietnam War with Walter Cronkite*.

23. *Public Papers of the Presidents: Johnson, 1968–69*, (Washington, DC: Government Printing Office, 1970), I: 122.

24. *Public Papers of the Presidents: Johnson, 1968–69*, I:155–61.

25. *Public Papers of the Presidents: Johnson, 1968–69*, I:155–61.

26. Godfrey Hodgson, *America in Our Time: From World War II to Nixon, What Happened and Why* (New York: Vintage, 1976), 356.

27. Oberdorfer, *TET!*, 176.

28. George Donelson Moss, *A Vietnam Reader: Sources and Essays* (Englewood Cliffs, NJ: Prentice Hall, 1991), 279.

29. Jorden to Rostow, February 3, 1968, NSF: CO Vietnam, Box 62, LBJL.

30. Quoted in Miles to Westmoreland, November 17, 1970, Gibbons Papers, Box 36, LBJL.

31. Oral History, Harry McPherson, LBJL.

32. Westmoreland to Wheeler, February 4, 1968, Gibbons Papers, Box 35, LBJL.

33. Johnson to Bunker, February 3, 1968, NSF: CO Vietnam, Box 62, LBJL.

34. Westmoreland to Wheeler, February 9, 1968, Gibbons Papers, Box 35, LBJL.

35. Notes of the President's Meeting with the Joint Chiefs of Staff, February 9, 1968, Gibbons Papers, Box 35, LBJL.

36. Notes of the President's Meeting with the Joint Chiefs of Staff, February 9, 1968, Gibbons Papers, Box 35, LBJL.

37. Westmoreland to Wheeler, February 12, 1968, Gibbons Papers, Box 35, LBJL.

38. Notes of the President's Meeting with Senior Foreign Policy Advisors, February 12, 1968, Gibbons Papers, Box 35, LBJL.

39. Hughes to Rusk, February 29, 1968, Gibbons Papers, Box 35, LBJL.

40. Hughes to Rusk, February 29, 1968, Gibbons Papers, Box 35, LBJL.

41. Smith to Helms, "The Outlook in Vietnam," February 26, 1968, NSF: CO Vietnam, Box 75, LBJL.

42. *Public Papers of the Presidents: Johnson 1968–69*, I:238–41.

43. Robert Buzzanco, *Masters of War: Military Dissent and Politics in the Vietnam Era* (New York: Cambridge University Press, 1996), 323.

44. Wheeler to Johnson, "Military Situation and Requirements in South Vietnam," February 27, 1968, NSF: CO Vietnam, Box 75, LBJL.

45. Report of Chairman, JCS on Situation in Vietnam and MACV Force Requirements, February 27, 1968, NSF: CO Vietnam, Box 75, LBJL.

46. Buzzanco, *Masters of War*, 311.

47. Wheeler to Johnson, "Military Situation and Requirements in South Vietnam," February 27, 1968, NSF: CO Vietnam, Box 75, LBJL.

48. Report of Chairman, JCS on Situation in Vietnam and MACV Force Requirements, February 27, 1968, NSF: CO Vietnam, Box 75, LBJL.

49. Observations on the Situation in Viet-Nam, February 26, 1968, NSF: CO Vietnam, Box 75, LBJL.

50. Report of Chairman, JCS on Situation in Vietnam and MACV Force Requirements, February 27, 1968, NSF: CO Vietnam, Box 75, LBJL.

51. Buzzanco, *Masters of War*, 325.

52. Video, "The Tet Offensive," *The Vietnam War with Walter Cronkite*.

53. Embassy Saigon to Rusk, February 26, 1968, NSF: CO Vietnam, Box 100, LBJL.

54. Cohen, *Vietnam*, 214–15.

55. Oberdorfer, *TET!*, 265.

56. Cohen, *Vietnam*, 214–15.

57. *The Gallup Poll*, III, 2109; *Gallup Opinion Index No. 35* (Princeton: Gallup International, 1968), 1.

58. Oberdorfer, *TET!*, 264.

59. Ackley to Johnson, "Economic Aspects of Vietnam," July 30, 1965, WHCF: National Security-Defense, Box 216, LBJL (emphasis in the original).

60. Hodgson, *America in Our Time*, 245.

61. Hodgson, *America in Our Time*, 246 (emphasis in the original).

62. Hodgson, *America in Our Time*, 53.

63. Rostow to Johnson, "How the System Works Now," February 14, 1968, NSF: NSC Histories, Gold Crisis, Box 53, LBJL.

64. "The Gold Market," December 24, 1967, NSF: NSC Histories, Gold Crisis, Box 53, LBJL.

65. Ackley to Johnson, January 24, 1968, NSF: NSC Histories, Gold Crisis, Box 53, LBJL (emphasis in the original).

66. Rostow to Johnson, February 14, 1968, "Where We are on Gold," NSF: NSC Histories, Gold Crisis, Box 53, LBJL.

67. Rostow to Johnson, March 9, 1968, NSF: NSC Histories, Gold Crisis, Box 53, LBJL.

68. Anthony S. Campagna, *The Economic Consequences of the Vietnam War* (New York: Praeger, 1991), 42.

69. Fowler to Johnson, "Gold Problems," March 4, 1968; Rostow to Johnson, March 14, 1968; and "The Gold Crisis, Nov.

1967–March 1968," NSF: NSC Histories, Gold Crisis, Box 53, LBJL.

70. Okun to Johnson, March 23, 1968, NSF: NSC Histories, Gold Crisis, Box 53, LBJL.

71. Oberdorfer, *TET!*, 192, 293.

72. Senator Gravel Edition, *The Pentagon Papers: The Defense Department History of United States Decisionmaking on Vietnam* (Boston: Beacon Press, 1971), IV: 549. (Emphasis in original).

73. Rostow to Clifford and Rusk, February 28, 1968, NSF: CO Vietnam, Box 75, LBJL.

74. Senator Gravel Edition, *The Pentagon Papers*, IV: 549.

Chapter Four

CAPPING ESCALATION

THE MARCH 1968 DEBATES WITHIN THE JOHNSON administration, which began with Clark Clifford's task force on the troop request and culminated with Lyndon Johnson's speech to the nation on March 31, were the turning point in the Vietnam War. The Tet Offensive created an atmosphere and space for alternative and dissenting views on the war in the State Department, CIA, and Department of Defense to be heard by the senior officials in the administration. As the pressure for more troops collided with the skeptical analysis of numerous officials, increasing awareness of the enemy's strength, and the full extent of the problems faced in Vietnam on the one hand, and the mounting unpopularity of the war and President Johnson, the widening credibility gap, and growing economic problems in the nation on the other hand, the establishment consensus on Vietnam broke.

Events moved quickly, from the shock when *The New York Times* published the news of the troop request to Senator Eugene McCarthy's near upset win in New Hampshire and Senator Robert Kennedy's decision to enter the presidential race, to the Wise Men shifting their position away from support of the war. In the center of it all was President Lyndon Johnson, watching his hopes for the Great Society and dreams for the nation sink into the rice paddies of Vietnam. He tried to rally support for the war and to hold on because it was almost impossible for him to accept that the decisions he had made were wrong and that America could not succeed in its effort to maintain a noncommunist government in Saigon. But as he saw the nation dividing over the war, and his most trusted advisors questioning the merits of his policy in Southeast Asia, Johnson decided that a change of course in Vietnam was necessary, and that he was too divisive a figure to lead the nation without creating further divisions and unrest. In the end, the internal review of American policy prompted by the Tet Offensive led to the capping of the American escalation of the war, a partial bombing halt of the North in the hopes of starting negotiations, and President Johnson's decision not to seek reelection.

THE CLIFFORD TASK FORCE

On February 29, Clifford met with his task force, which included Secretary of State Dean Rusk, Secretary of the Treasury Henry Fowler, Assistant Undersecretary of State Nicholas Katzenbach, Deputy Secretary of Defense Paul Nitze, General Wheeler, Walt Whitman Rostow, Richard Helms, Bill Bundy, and General Taylor, to outline their work and prepare for their meetings over the next three days. The key issue to be considered was not whether to send 200,000 more troops as requested. As the authors of the *Pentagon Papers* note, the questions to be addressed, according to Clifford, were: "Should we follow the present course in SVN:

could it ever prove successful even if vastly more than 200,000 troops were sent?" Answering these questions and looking at different courses of action would be the focus of the inquiry.[1] What Clifford and others learned in the process was in striking contrast to the information senior officials and the Wise Men heard in the fall of 1967. When the intense and exhaustive meetings were over, Clifford recalled that "I had turned against the war."[2]

The CIA reports that were used by Clifford's task force in its reassessment of policy presented a bleak picture of the situation in South Vietnam. One paper, entitled "The Outlook in Vietnam," stated that "the Communists will sustain a high level of military activity for at least the next two or three months" and that neither side "will be capable of registering decisive gains."[3] Addressing the specific questions put to it by Clifford concerning the course of the war over the next year and the impact of additional American troops, the CIA concluded that the war would remain a stalemate. Just as it was "impossible for the Communists to drive US forces out of the country," it was "out of the question for US/GVN forces to clear South Vietnam of Communist forces." While the war could take a decisive turn in the next ten months, it was "unlikely that this turn could be in the US/GVN favor." "Far more likely is an erosion of the ARVN's morale and effectiveness." While the Saigon government would not collapse, "virtually the entire burden of the war would fall on US forces." In summary, "the overall situation 10 months hence will be no better than a standoff."[4]

Escalation would not produce any change in this situation. Rather, the enemy would match the increase with one of its own and continue the war. "They still have resources available in North Vietnam and within South Vietnam to increase their troop strength." The National Liberation Front's (NLF) "logistical effort and their ability to organize and exploit the people under their control in the South enable them to counter US increases by smaller increases of their own." Along with recruitment in the South, Hanoi would be able "to introduce sufficient new units into the South to offset the US maneuver battalion increments" of 100,000 or 200,000 troops. In other words, the stalemate would continue.[5]

Equally troubling were the papers prepared by the Office of International Security Affairs (ISA) in the Department of Defense that concluded that more troops "would not achieve decisive results and, indeed, would not be satisfactory." On the question of pacification, the ISA found that the program had actually "lost ground in the second half" of 1967. The gains reported were "results from accounting changes" in the Hamlet Evaluation System "not from pacification progress." Most importantly, the "enemy's current offensive appears to have killed the program once and for all."[6]

Other statistical assessments of progress were also questioned, as were the basic assumptions of U.S. objectives in South Vietnam. "We became mesmerized by statistics of known doubtful validity," such as body counts, troop strength, and attrition, "choosing to place our faith only in the ones that showed progress." The setbacks suffered since the Tet Offensive "were due to wishful thinking compounded by a massive intelligence collection and/or evaluation failure." Further American escalation held no promise for any improvement as the enemy "shows no lack of capability or will to match each new US escalation. Our strategy of attrition has not worked." Moreover, the United States had failed to meet any of its objectives in terms of making it too costly for the NLF and North Vietnamese Army (NVA) to continue, extending the control of Saigon over the population, or defeating the Viet Cong and forcing the withdrawal of Northern troops. On the contrary, "the TET offensive proves we were further from this goal than we thought." In conclusion, the Office of International Security Affairs stated: "we know that despite a massive influx of 500,000 US troops, 1.2 million tons of bombs a year, 400,000 attack sorties per year, 200,000 enemy KIA in three years, 20,000 US KIA, etc., our control of the countryside and the defense of the urban areas is now essentially at pre-August 1965 levels. We have achieved stalemate at a high commitment."[7] That meant that despite the air war and two and a half years of ground fighting by American forces, no progress had been made toward victory.

The ISA Office also examined increased troop commitments from the viewpoint of the public's reaction. A simple increase with no change in any aspect of American policy would evoke an "extremely negative" response. The deployment of significant numbers of new troops along with increased bombing would bring a "campus and liberal reaction [that] would surpass anything we have seen." An increased deployment combined with bombing pause "would be more favorably received" since it would "offer more hope of an eventual solution to the war." But doves would still deplore the escalation of ground forces and the nation would remain badly divided. A fourth option of denying the troop request and continuing the war as it was being fought prior to Tet "would please no one." The overwhelmingly most popular option would be the denial of the troop request and a change in strategy in South Vietnam. Of the five options, this was the only one that was considered acceptable from the point of view of the public's response. It would eliminate the additional costs of "Reserve callups, increased draft calls, increased casualties, extended tours," and the dangers of increased bombings. "The frustration of more–and–more–and–more into the endless pit would be eliminated" as well. "What the people want most of all is some sign that we *are* making progress, that there is, somewhere, an end. While this does not necessarily show progress, it does show change. It does show the search for new approaches."[8]

These reports, in Clifford's words, provided a "ruthlessly frank assessment of our situation by the men who knew the most about it." The principal issues raised during the meetings of the task force, and Clifford's meetings with the Joint Chiefs of Staff, were centered on the fundamental questions of American strategy in Vietnam. The new secretary of defense set out the questions he raised, the impressions he formed, and the conclusions he drew over three days of meetings in an article published the next year in *Foreign Affairs*.

"Will 200,000 more men do the job?" I found no assurance that they would.

"If not, how many more might be needed—and when?" There was no way of knowing. . . .

"Can the enemy respond with a build-up of his own?" He could and he probably would.

"What are the estimated costs of the latest requests?" First calculations were on the order of $2 billion for the remaining four months of that fiscal year, and an increase of $10 to $12 billion for the year beginning July 1, 1968.

"What will be the impact on the economy?" So great that we would face the possibility of credit restrictions, a tax increase and even wage and price controls. The balance of payments would be worsened by at least half a billion dollars a year.

"Can bombing stop the war?" Never by itself. It was inflicting heavy personnel and material losses, but bombing by itself would not stop the war. . . .

"How long must we keep on sending our men and carrying the main burden of combat?" The South Vietnamese were doing better, but they were not ready yet to replace our troops and we did not know when they would be.

When Clifford asked how the United States could win, he was told it would occur by continuing "to evidence our superiority over the enemy; we would continue to attack in the belief that he would reach the stage where he would find it inadvisable to go on with the war. He could not afford the attrition we were inflicting on him." How long would this take, he asked, six months, a year, two years? "There was no agreement on an answer. Not only was there no agreement," Clifford wrote, "I could find no one willing to express any confidence in his guesses. Certainly, none of us was willing to assert that he could see 'light at the end of the tunnel' or that American troops would be coming home by the end of the year."[9]

The secretary of defense then asked, does "anyone see any diminution in the will of the enemy after four years of our having been there, after enormous casualties and after massive destruction from our bombing?" The answer was no. "This reply was doubly impressive," Clifford recalled, when put into the context of rising domestic unrest and the "economic implications of a struggle to be indefinitely continued at ever-increasing cost." He noted that the "dollar was already in trouble, prices were escalating far too fast," and "more stringent economic controls" would be necessary if another $12 billion in spending on Vietnam was added. The United States had other obligations, and "we could not afford to disregard our interests in the Middle East, South Asia, Africa, Western Europe and elsewhere." Even if one accepted the validity of American policy in Vietnam, as Clifford had up to this point, "that objective had to be viewed in the context of our overall national interest, and could not sensibly be pursued at a price so high as to impair our ability to achieve other, and perhaps even more important, foreign policy objectives."[10]

With no assurance that the requested increase in American troops would improve the military situation in South Vietnam, Clifford concluded "that the military course we were pursuing was not only endless, but hopeless." A 40 percent increase in American forces "could only increase the devastation and the Americanization of the war." The primary goal now "should be to level off our involvement, and to work toward gradual disengagement."[11] The former hawk and prominent supporter of the war in the fall of 1967 had concluded that the war was a mistake. His task now, as he saw it, was to convince President Johnson to change course.

On March 4, Clifford forwarded his draft memorandum of the task force's recommendations to the president along with eight attached papers that set out the evidence and reasoning behind their conclusion. The memorandum began by reviewing the troop request and outlining its impact in terms of reserve call-ups, increased draft calls, and the extension of tours of duty that would be necessary to meet it. The task force supported immediately sending 22,000 additional troops and applying renewed pressure on Saigon for a greater effort in the war. It put on hold the decision to meet the full request and a decision on bombing policy, to await further developments and until more studies could be conducted on possible alternative courses of action "in the context of our world-wide politico-military strategy."[12] Rostow told Johnson that everyone "agreed that there should be a fresh review of our strategy" in Vietnam "before you are asked to make a commitment to send [Westmoreland] forces" beyond those recommended by the task force.[13]

The case for further study was set out in the appendix entitled "Necessity for In-Depth Study of Vietnam Policy and Strategic Guidance," which addressed the major points of Clifford's task force. It had to be recognized, the report stated, that Westmoreland's request did not provide a solution to the problem in Vietnam. "There can be no assurance that this very substantial additional deployment would leave us a year from today in any more favorable military

Swearing in of Clark Clifford as Secretary of Defense, March 1, 1968.

position." All that was certain was that it would increase the level of violence and number of casualties, and that the "increased Americanization of the war could, in fact, be counter-productive." It might lead to a wider war and a major conflict with the Soviet Union and/or China, spread American resources so thin "that our other world-wide commitments—especially NATO—are no longer credible," and create doubts in attitudes of the American public "such that our other commitments are brought into question as a matter of US will."[14]

The change in NVA and NLF tactics, their willingness and ability to commit more forces to the fighting, and "the obvious and not wholly anticipated strength of the Viet Cong infrastructure, shows that there can be no prospect of a quick military solution to the aggression in South Vietnam." In these circumstances, intensive study was needed to develop new strategies toward the war. The cost of destroying enemy forces and driving them out of South Vietnam was impossible to estimate, and "there is no reason to believe that it could be done by an additional 200,000 American troops or double or triple that quantity."[15]

There was also uncertainty, Rostow wrote Johnson, about what new troops would be used for. "We don't know whether we are being asked to send forces to prevent a radical deterioration in our side's position, or to permit [Westmoreland] to conduct in the second half of the year a vigorous offensive." The reservations against sending more troops "which goes deep in State and Defense, is that the additional forces would constitute a gross over-commitment of U.S. military resources to Viet Nam without bringing us closer to a resolution of the problem." Underlining that position was a view "that we can only attain our objectives in Viet Nam by a negotiation which brings the Viet Cong into the political process." This would not be advanced by a major American escalation.[16]

In brief, escalation would not bring victory, but it would increase the costs of the war and the internal divisions within the nation. The task force concluded that the resulting debate from an approval of the troop request would be "prolonged and divisive," and would have a profoundly negative economic impact within the nation. Secretary Fowler was emphatic that the necessary increases in "expenditures must be met by 1–for–1 tax" or spending cuts elsewhere "to avoid serious effects on the domestic economy and the stability of the dollar." In an election year, however, further tax increases were doubtful even if matched by new cuts in domestic programs. All of this would widen the credibility gap and increase the distrust concerning what the administration said about the war. In the fall, the task force noted, the administration was claiming victory, and now it would be saying that Westmoreland needs significant help.[17]

At a meeting with the president that evening, Clifford carefully set out the task force's recommendations and rationale for more study. Concerning escalation, Clifford declared that "we seem to have a sinkhole. We put in more—they match it. We put in more—they match it." All it meant was more intense fighting and more casualties with "no end in sight to the action." It was not possible just to keep meeting every troop request made by Westmoreland. "We can no longer rely just on the field commander" for these considerations, Clifford stated. "We must look at our economic stability, our other problems in the world, our other problems at home; we must consider whether this thing is tieing [sic] us down so that we cannot do some of the other things we should be doing." It was unclear, Clifford concluded, whether any progress was being made. More than likely, the war was a stalemate and the costs were getting to be more than the nation could afford. Johnson agreed with the recommendation to send the 22,000 troops and to delay action on the rest of the request until a more complete examination of the question could be completed.[18]

It was Wheeler's job to inform Westmoreland of the decision. The chairman of the Joint Chiefs of Staff explained to him "that there is strong resistance from all quarters to putting more ground units in South Vietnam. The call-up of reserves and the concomitant actions that must be taken will raise unshirted hell in many influential quarters." He wanted Westmoreland to know that while the decision on sending more troops was officially still under study, he "should not count upon and [sic] affirmative decision for such additional forces." The most important figure in the discussions was Secretary of Defense Clifford, who Wheeler portrayed as a man of great stature, "very astute, intelligent and able," and who "is closely in touch with Congressional leaders, the business community, and the heads of the news media." As Westmoreland undoubtedly knew, "he has been the trusted advisor to four presidents" and a man "whose views must be accorded weight." Clifford, Wheeler reported, was very worried about the declining support for the war among business leaders and the growing credibility gap in the nation. All this, from Clifford's view, made escalation impossible.[19]

Rostow was the most important exception to Wheeler's summary of opposition from all quarters. The national security advisor continued to see Tet as a major victory, remained optimistic about the war, and supported sending more troops. To counter Clifford's opposition and influence, he sent a steady stream of messages to Johnson designed to lift the president's spirits and bolster his resolve to stay with the war. Some of these were historical analogies, while others drew on the verities of the Cold War. During the discussions on the troop request, Rostow forwarded to Johnson what he termed a "comforting historical memorandum relating to the Communist Tet offensive." It argued that in three past major wars the United States fought, World War II, World War I, and the Civil War, the "losing side threw everything it had into one last all-out offensive," the Battle of the Bulge, the German spring 1918 offensive, and the Battle of Atlanta, and "the winning side was psychologically discombobulated by same; the net effect was to hasten the end of the war." This analysis suggested that there "may be a law of human nature" that "prompts the losing side to take large risks and losses in a last offensive . . . just before its collapse" and in the process "conceals from the winning side the degree of the enemy's desperation and the extent to which, despite tactical successes, the enemy's offensive has hastened his ultimate defeat."[20]

After the task force recommendations, Rostow urged Johnson not to lose faith and to move forward in Vietnam to make 1968 the year of victory. The objective was to "produce a situation in which Hanoi decided to end the war." While he acknowledged that "we are clearly in the midst of an unresolved critical battle," Rostow contended that "there is no evidence [the enemy] can sustain present rates for more than a matter of a few months." The United States, therefore, "must behave in the days ahead in a way to make clear we have the will and staying power to carry on." Once the battles in the northern provinces were decided, "assuming some tactical success in the forthcoming battles," Rostow recommended a reserve call-up, a mining of the harbors of North Vietnam, and an offer to begin peace negotiations. "Not since the Civil War," Rostow opined, "has quite so much hinged for our country on immediate battlefield events."[21] In support of his recommendations, he forwarded to Johnson the weekly optimistic appraisals of the Tet Offensive and the military situation in Vietnam by Ambassador Bunker, which emphasized the number of enemy forces killed, their failure to hold any cities and inability to spark an uprising, and plans from Westmoreland on how he was preparing "to move out on the offensive."[22]

Rostow consistently framed the decisions to be made as coming "at a most important moment in postwar history." It was essential, he believed, to maintain the American commitment in Vietnam and push forward to victory. Invoking the notion of monolithic communism and the domino theory, Rostow wrote Johnson that "if we lose our heads at this critical moment and listen to extremists, we might destroy the basis for the resistance to aggression in Southeast Asia; open the way to a new phase of Communist expansion . . . and bring us all much closer to a third world war." There was, Rostow insisted, "no reason to despair in Vietnam." American forces would get through the Tet Offensive on top, and with a renewed vigor in Saigon, "the picture could look quite different by the end of May than it does right now. Our own forces are in excellent shape. But this is a battle to be fought. We have half a million Americans to back, as fully as we can, in the days ahead. That is our first duty."[23] This debate over troops and the course of the war would continue until the end of the month.

POLITICAL SHOCKS

On Sunday, March 10, two days before the New Hampshire primary, the *New York Times* broke the news that Westmoreland had requested 206,000 more American troops and that the request had set off a divisive debate within the Johnson administration. The *Times* report was remarkably accurate on the exact request, the costs it would entail, and the arguments against the increase. The story noted that military leaders sought an increase to regain the initiative and "permit the allied forces to resume the pacification of the countryside and the war of attrition against the Vietcong that they contend was being successfully waged before the Tet offensive." The argument against the request was that the escalation would be matched by Hanoi and "would simply raise the level of violence. The United States would spend billions more on the war effort and would suffer appreciably higher casualties" just to maintain a stalemate. The president, it was noted, had not yet reached a decision on the issue and had requested "extensive staff studies of the full political, economic and political ramifications of giving General Westmoreland more troops."[24]

The nation was still in the midst of sorting out what the troop request meant when the voters in New Hampshire went to the polls and delivered the second shock in three days. Eugene McCarthy received 42.4 percent of the Democratic Party vote for the presidency along with a number of crossover write-in votes from Republicans. When taken together, he lost to President Johnson by only 230 votes, or less than one percentage point of the vote.[25] New Hampshire voters had mixed reasons for casting their ballots for McCarthy. For some it was a peace vote, for others it was a way to register their dissatisfaction with President Johnson and the state of the war. They wanted to win or get out. Whatever their motivations, it was clear that the discontent in the nation over the war, as McGeorge Bundy had noted in November 1967, was "wide and deep," and that people were

not seeing any progress that would alter that fact. With Mc-
Carthy now a legitimate antiwar candidate, the president's
political fortunes were in trouble. Projections for the next
primary in Wisconsin indicated that McCarthy would defeat
Johnson there by as wide as a two to one margin.[26]

McCarthy's stunning achievement opened the door for
Robert Kennedy to announce his candidacy on March 16.
Kennedy, who had earlier broken with the administration
over the war, had been the original choice of many of the antiwar activists who were supporting McCarthy. He had hesitated and then decided not to run, unsure of the wisdom of
challenging an incumbent president. Now he joined the race
confident that the president could be defeated and, with the
Kennedy name, support from civil rights organizations, la-
bor, and liberals, that he could secure the nomination. He
believed that the Tet Offensive "finally shattered the mask of
official illusion with which we have concealed our true circumstances." The nation had to rid itself of the illusions
that the events since the attacks on the cities "represent some
sort of victory," that progress was being made, and that "the
unswerving pursuit of military victory, whatever its cost, is
in the interest of either ourselves or the people of Vietnam."
Rather, Kennedy declared, the Tet Offensive "carries with it
some basic truths," most notably that a "total military victory is not within sight or around the corner; that, in fact, it
is probably beyond our grasp; and that the effort to win such
a victory will only result in the further slaughter of thousands of innocent and helpless people." The continued escalation of the fighting was not making the nation more
secure, but undercutting its credibility in the world and "reducing the faith of other peoples in our wisdom and purpose and weakening the world's resolve to stand together
for freedom and peace." The only way out was a negotiated

political compromise that showed "as much willingness to risk some of our prestige for peace as to risk the lives of young men in war."[27]

In the face of these challenges, Johnson was publicly defiant. Speaking in Minneapolis on March 18, he set out the familiar narrative of post–World War II history that provided the logic and rationale for containment and American policy in Vietnam. Since 1945, Johnson declared, the United States had been engaged in a struggle "to stop the on-rushing tide of Communist aggression." What was faced in Greece, Berlin, Korea, and elsewhere was now being met in Southeast Asia. The United States, the president assured his audience, was fighting to defend freedom and the right of nations to govern themselves. "We seek that right and we will—make no mistake about it—win." Everyone wanted peace, Johnson noted, but it could not be bought at the price of appeasing aggression. "Wanting peace, praying for peace, and desiring peace, as Chamberlain found out, doesn't always give you peace." The United States should not let Hanoi "win something in Washington that they can't win in Hue, in the I Corps, or in Khe Sanh. And we are not going to."[28]

The next day, Johnson claimed that what was being tested in Vietnam was not U.S. power, but "the will of America." There could be no doubt about it, Johnson stated: the Tet Offensive was "aimed squarely at the citizens of America. It is an assault that is designed to crack America's will." The communists sought more than to just conquer South Vietnam or the collapse of all of Southeast Asia. They struck "at the right of any man or any nation to live with its neighbors without fear, to find its own destiny, and to determine for itself." It was the duty and the obligation of the United States to stand up and protect small nations in order to protect itself. "We must not break our commitment

for freedom and for the future of the world," Johnson concluded. "We have set our course. We will pursue it just as
long as aggression threatens it. And make no mistake about
it—America will prevail."[29]

The president was equally determined in private as
well. He told South Vietnam's Ambassador to the United
States Bui Diem that although criticism of the war was rising in the nation and he was under intense pressure, "he was
firm in his conviction of the rightness of our course in Viet-
Nam." He assured the ambassador that he would ask Congress and the American people "for additional sacrifice and
expenditures." In return, he expected "the Vietnamese to
bear a heavier load, too." The ambassador needed to tell
President Thieu and Vice President Nguyen Cao Ky to
"work together and get moving."[30] In support of his words,
Johnson finalized the sending of the 22,000 troops agreed
to by the task force on March 4.[31]

There were indications, however, that Johnson was not
as sure of his course of action as these statements suggested.
He still had not approved the request for 200,000 more
troops, and every indication was that he would not grant it.
All of his political instincts told him that the economic
costs and the political price, internationally and domesti-
cally, were too great to pay on a proposition with so little
promise. As his staff was beginning to prepare a major presidential speech on the war, he agreed with Clifford's suggestion that he reconvene the Wise Men to get their opinions
on what course he should take in Vietnam. Finally, on March
22, in what amounted to a vote of no confidence and a sig-
nal that he was thinking of taking a different course, Johnson announced that General Westmoreland would leave his
command in Vietnam that summer to become the Army
Chief of Staff.

WISE MEN II

Clifford recommended calling back the senior group of advisors known as the Wise Men because "after Tet . . . there was no suggestion that we could see any light at the end of the tunnel, nor was there any thought of sending any American boys home. The whole thrust was exactly the reverse." The nation was "going through this rather difficult debate" and it seemed prudent to ascertain "whether or not Tet had had the impact on these men that I knew it had had on me and had on some others within the administration." They would provide a benchmark for the president on attitudes toward the war.[32]

The same group that had met in early November 1967, with the addition of General Matthew Ridgway and Cyrus Vance, former Deputy Secretary of Defense and a New York attorney, gathered for dinner on Monday evening, March 25. Along with papers from Clifford's task force and other documents, they received oral reports from members of the State Department, CIA, and the Department of Defense on the request for an increase in U.S. force strength, bombing policy, the military situation, enemy capabilities and plans, the internal political situation in Saigon, and the status of possible negotiations.[33] They were told that Thieu's government was weaker than previously believed, that conditions in the South were worse due to the Tet Offensive, and that there was a dispute between Defense and the CIA, which went back to the previous year, over enemy strength. While both acknowledged the enemy was stronger than what was reported in the fall, Defense's estimates still only counted identifiable military units while the CIA's "included all known military, paramilitary, and parttime enemy strength available." These presentations were markedly different than

Second meeting of the Wise Men, March 26, 1968. Clockwise from head of table, General Creighton Abrams, General Earle Wheeler, George Ball, Tom Johnson, Maxwell Taylor, McGeorge Bundy, Matthew Ridgway, Arthur Dean, Henry Cabot Lodge, Dean Acheson, President Lyndon B. Johnson, Omar Bradley, Averill Harriman, Robert Murphy, Clark Clifford, Douglas Dillon, Cyrus Vance, Walt Whitman Rostow, Arthur Goldberg, Dean Rusk.

the ones the Wise Men had received in the fall and presented the war as a stalemate with little prospect for improvement in the near future. As General Ridgway put it, the briefings were "gloomy, but, on the whole, factual."[34]

On March 26, the senior advisors met in the morning to discuss the reports, briefing papers they were supplied, and their thoughts, and to arrive at their recommendations for the president. When they met with Johnson after lunch, McGeorge Bundy acted as rapporteur for the group. He told the president that "there is a very significant shift in our position. When we last met we saw reasons for hope." Given the information presented then, they thought "there would be slow but steady progress. Last night and today the picture is not so hopeful particularly in the countryside." A continued escalation of American forces and/or greater bombing would not succeed. Bundy continued by noting that Dean Acheson had best summed up the "majority feeling when he said that we can no longer do the job we set out to do in the time we have left and we must begin to take steps to disengage."[35] Everyone agreed that efforts should be made to strengthen the government in Saigon, but the majority thought that there "should not be an increase in force levels in South Vietnam and there should be a modification of the policy of bombing North Vietnam" designed to begin the process of finding a political solution to the war through negotiations.[36]

Concerning reenforcements, "the dominant sentiment was that the burden of proof rests with those who are urging the increase." They feared that such a move would not have any positive impact and could possibly lead to a wider conflict that "would be against our national interest." This was a dramatic turnaround from 1965 when the "burden of proof" rested on the shoulders of George Ball to demonstrate an American escalation would not succeed. As the former undersecretary of state said, "I have felt that way since 1961—that our objectives are not attainable." Acheson told Johnson that he agreed with everything Bundy said. "Neither the effort of the Government of Vietnam or the effort of the U.S. government can succeed in the time we have left." That time was "limited by reactions in this country. We cannot build an independent South Vietnam: therefore, we should do something by no later than late summer to establish something different."[37]

There were a few—Robert Murphy, General Taylor, and Abe Fortas—who dissented from the dramatically changed view that the troops should not be sent, and that changes be made to the bombing policy connected to starting negotiations and beginning a disengagement of the United States from Vietnam. Murphy stated that he was "shaken by the position of my associates" and cast this approach as a "give-away" policy. Taylor did not want to "concede the home front: let's do something about it." Fortas argued that the goal had never been a military victory in the traditional sense, but to protect South Vietnam and maintain a noncommunist government in Saigon by forcing Hanoi "to reach an agreement or settle for the status quo between North Vietnam and South Vietnam." Acheson responded by stating the issue at hand was not the one Fortas set out. "The issue is can we do what we are trying to do in Vietnam. I do not think we can. . . . The issue is can we by military means keep the North Vietnamese off the South Vietnamese. I do not think we can."[38]

The president was stunned by what he heard and said that he "would like to hear from the men who had briefed" the Wise Men as they "seemed to have obtained information of a type which he had not been getting."[39] Indeed, the views of the Wise Men, particularly McGeorge Bundy and Dean Acheson, could not have been more different from the positions they took in the fall, and were much more negative presentations of the situation than Johnson had been receiving from Rostow. In November 1967, Johnson had gained support and renewed confidence in his policy from their advice. Now they were telling him it was all for naught, that the United States could not win. Bundy thought that Johnson had already decided not to send any more ground troops, but that the pessimism and gloominess of the group deeply troubled the president.[40]

As Clifford recalled, it was a "bitter pill" for the president.[41] "You could just sense it, it was just a great big swing all around from an almost unanimous belief in the rightness of our cause in the first group meeting and a substantial shift in the meeting of the second group." Now, Clifford said, the thrust "was that we should not continue to pour blood and treasure into Viet Nam but that we should give the most careful consideration to seeing if we couldn't find some way to negotiate ourselves out of Viet Nam." The majority of the Wise Men believed "that military pressure was not going to gain the disengagement which we really should begin to think about seriously."[42] The establishment consensus that Vietnam was a proper use of American power and that the United States could force North Vietnam and the NLF to accept American wishes had broken. With it, all of the logic and rationale for the war was gone for these men. It was not college students, demonstrators, or news people who influenced this shift, but their own examination of the evidence on the war and conclusion that it was an unwinnable stalemate. Still, as Clifford noted, it was fine that he and the others had changed their minds, but the opinion that really mattered was Lyndon Johnson's.[43]

CODA

Since the earliest days of the Tet Offensive, the Johnson administration discussed having the president deliver a major speech to the nation on the war in order to provide an assessment of Tet and to reassure the public. The earliest drafts of the speech were similar in tone to the talks Johnson gave in the middle of March: determined, calling on the people for more sacrifices, justifying the costs in lives and money the war had already claimed, and promising to persevere to the end to save Vietnam. Clifford set out to change the tone and approach of the speech, to use it as a means of altering the direction of American policy. In a meeting with Rusk, Rostow, Bill Bundy, and speech writer Harry McPherson, the secretary of defense told them that it was impossible to continue with the current policy, that the leaders in business and the legal profession, due to the economic problems it was creating, had given up on the war. He said, "those guys who have been with us and who have sustained us so far as we are sustained are no longer with us." The address to the nation, he continued, "as it is presently written, is wrong. The speech is more of the same. The American people are fed up with more of the same . . . because more of the same means no win, and only a continual long drag on American resources." What the United States needed to do, Clifford stated, was find a way to begin a disengagement from the war. A quest for a military victory was a dead end. The war was a stalemate and it could not be won. Escalation would be matched by the enemy and the sending of more troops to Vietnam was "going to just be more American boys killed." The current draft "was a speech about war," Clifford concluded, "and what . . . the President should do was make a speech about peace."[44]

McPherson had already sent Johnson a memorandum with a proposal to halt the bombing of North Vietnam above the 20th parallel as a step to get negotiations started. The logic was that this would free 90 percent of North Vietnam's population and most of its territory from air attacks while still allowing bombing in the staging areas most important for protecting American troops. Rusk endorsed the idea as "a possible peace move," as did most of the Wise Men, and it received Bunker's assurance that the military in Saigon and Thieu's government would go along with such a step. To Clifford, this was "enormously important" because he did not believe President Johnson would make such an important change without Rusk's support. McPherson prepared a new draft of the speech incorporating this idea and the change in approach that the group had discussed, and sent it to Johnson with a note telling him that "this is what your advisers think you ought to say."[45]

With the economy still in trouble, divisions deepening in the country and the Democratic Party, and most of his advisors urging him to adopt a new approach to the war, Johnson finally decided not to send the troops requested at the end of February. It was clear from Wheeler's most recent report that there was little hope for success in the near future in Vietnam. The Saigon government, he told the National Security Council on March 27, was "frozen" and unable to take action because "the VC had established a stranglehold around the cities." Thieu was unwilling to have his troops leave the cities "since he felt the government simply could not afford another Tet offensive." While there was no fear of suffering "a major defeat in South Vietnam," neither were there any signs of victory.[46] A new ceiling was set at 549,500 troops. This would allow for a final 13,500 in support forces to join the 11,000 troops dispatched that month. There, however, would be no more beyond this.[47] At the same time, Johnson informed McPherson that he liked the alternative draft, including the idea of a partial bombing halt, as the basis for his speech.

On Sunday, March 31 at 9 p.m. Eastern Standard Time, Johnson spoke to the nation. The change in tone of the speech was evident from the opening sentence. The old draft had begun, "I wish to talk about the war in Vietnam." The speech Johnson delivered started with "I want to speak to you of peace in Vietnam and Southeast Asia." After a quick summary of previous offers to begin negotia-

President Johnson addresses the nation from the Oval Office, March 31, 1968.

tions and a section on the failure of the enemy to achieve any of its objectives during the Tet Offensive, Johnson turned to the central points of his speech. He announced to the nation that in the hopes of getting talks started, "I am taking the first step to de-escalate the conflict. We are reducing—substantially reducing—the present level of hostilities. And we are doing so unilaterally, and at once." Johnson continued: "I have ordered our aircraft and our naval vessels to make no attacks on North Vietnam, except in the area north of the Demilitarized Zone where the continuing enemy build-up directly threatens allied forward positions and where the movements of their troops and supplies are clearly related to that threat." In order to begin negotiations as soon as possible, he designated the venerable Ambassador Averell Harriman as his personal representative for any talks.[48]

The president also announced his final troop increase of 13,500 men. He explained that these forces, along with the ones sent earlier in the month, would increase the cost of the war by over $2.5 billion and called upon Congress to pass the tax increases he asked for in order to meet these costs and address the growing budget deficit. The "failure to act and to act promptly and decisively would raise very strong doubt throughout the world about America's willingness to keep its financial house in order." This was creating the "sharpest financial threat in the postwar era—a threat to the dollar's role as the keystone of international trade and finance in the world."[49]

Johnson concluded the speech by invoking the words of Abraham Lincoln that "a house divided against itself by the spirit of faction, of party, of region, or religion, of race, is a house that cannot stand." There was, unfortunately, "division in the American house now" due to the war. Given this, Johnson produced his surprise ending to the speech. "I have concluded," he stated, "that I should not permit the Presidency to become involved in the partisan divisions that are developing in this political year. With America's sons in the fields far away, with America's future under challenge right here at home . . . I do not believe that I should devote an hour or a day of my time to any personal partisan causes or to any duties other than the awesome duties of this office—the Presidency of your country. Accordingly, I shall not seek, and I will not accept, the nomination of my party for another term as your President."[50]

Three days after the president's speech, the White House announced that North Vietnam was appointing representatives to meet with the United States, and in mid-May talks opened in Paris. On April 11, Clifford formally announced that the 206,000 men requested would not be sent and that the limit of all U.S. forces in Vietnam would be 550,000 troops. A major shift in policy had led to the first small steps to finding peace in Vietnam.

Johnson had once again faced a decision to escalate the war. This time, however, with the public wondering whether the war would ever end, the price in terms of blood and treasure increasing beyond anything the administration had foreseen, political divisions at home, and an emerging economic crisis, the president balked at the request of the military. To grant Westmoreland and the Joint Chiefs of Staff their wish would have meant putting over 700,000 troops in Vietnam with no guarantee that they would not have to be complemented further in the future or that increased military strength would work. The price of a military victory was too much. His most trusted advisors, particularly Clark Clifford, were against any greater commitment or expansion of the war. Moreover, Lyndon Johnson did not want to see the nation divided any further, and he did not want to be the cause of that division. As Johnson later said, he wanted to keep the presidency out of the campaign. "I'm not that pure. I am that scared. The situation of the country is critical."[51]

Steady progress in building the nation of South Vietnam and defeating the NLF insurgency had been promised in 1965 and claimed from then on. The Tet Offensive demonstrated that this progress was illusory. The result was an "A to Z" reevaluation of American policy in Vietnam that led to a questioning of the original logic and purpose of American intervention into Vietnam. What the majority of Johnson's advisors, and ultimately the president himself, concluded was that a military victory was not possible under acceptable costs to the nation, and it was time to begin the process of getting the United States out of Vietnam. In two months, from the launching of the Tet Offensive to Johnson's decision not to seek reelection, American policy in Vietnam was changed from continual escalation designed to bring a military victory to a capping of escalation, partial suspension of the bombing, and unilateral action to start disengaging the United States from the war.

NOTES

1. Senator Gravel Edition, *The Pentagon Papers: The Defense Department History of United States Decisionmaking on Vietnam* (Boston: Beacon Press, 1971), IV: 549.

2. PBS, *Vietnam: A Television History*, Vol. 4, "Tet, 1968" (Boston: WGHB, 1985).

3. Office of National Estimates, "The Outlook in Vietnam," February 26, 1968, NSF: CO Vietnam, Box 75, LBJL.

4. CIA, "Questions Concerning the Situation in Vietnam," March 1, 1968, Clifford Papers, Box I, LBJL.

5. CIA, "Questions Concerning the Situation in Vietnam," March 1, 1968, Clifford Papers, Box I, LBJL.

6. Senator Gravel Edition, *The Pentagon Papers*, IV: 556.

7. Senator Gravel Edition, *The Pentagon Papers*, IV, 556–58.

8. Senator Gravel Edition, *The Pentagon Papers*, IV, 559–61 (emphasis in the original).

9. Clark Clifford, "A Viet Nam Reappraisal," *Foreign Affairs*, vol. 47, no. 4 (July 1969), 609–12.

10. Clifford, "A Viet Nam Reappraisal," 612–13.

11. Clifford, "A Viet Nam Reappraisal," 612–13.

12. Clifford, "Draft Memorandum for the President," March 4, 1968, NSF: CO Vietnam, Box 75, LBJL.

13. Rostow to Johnson, "The Clifford Committee," March 4, 1968, NSF: Memos to the President, Rostow, Box 30, LBJL.

14. "Necessity for In-Depth Study of Vietnam Policy and Strategic Guidance," March 4, 1968, Tab D, NSF: CO Vietnam, Box 75, LBJL.

15. "Necessity for In-Depth Study of Vietnam Policy and Strategic Guidance," March 4, 1968, Tab D, NSF: CO Vietnam, Box 75, LBJL.

16. Rostow to Johnson, "The Clifford Committee," March 4, 1968, NSF: Memos to the President, Rostow, Box 30, LBJL.

17. "Difficulties and Negative Factors in the Course of Action," and "Problems We Can Anticipate in U.S. Public Opinion," March 4, 1968, Tabs G and H, NSF: CO Vietnam, LBJL.

18. "Notes of the President's Meeting with Senior Foreign Policy Adviser's," March 4, 1968, Gibbons Papers, Box 36, LBJL.

19. Wheeler to Westmoreland, March 8, 1968, and March 9, 1968, Gibbons Papers, Box 36, LBJL.

20. Rostow to Johnson, February 28, 1968, NSF: Memos to the President, Rostow, Box 30, LBJL.

21. Rostow to Johnson, March 6, 1968, Gibbons Papers, Box 36, LBJL.

22. Rostow to Johnson, March 6, 1968, NSF: CO Vietnam, Box 76, LBJL; see also February 15, 1968, February 29, 1968, and March 14, 1968, NSF: NSC Histories, March 31st Speech, Box 48, LBJL.

23. Rostow to Johnson, March 15, 1968, NSF: Memos to the President, Rostow, Box 31, LBJL.

24. *New York Times*, March 10, 1968, 1.

25. Charles Kaiser, *1968 in America: Music, Politics, Chaos, Counterculture, and the Shaping of a Generation* (New York: Weidenfeld & Nicolson, 1988), 103.

26. Godfrey Hodgson, *America in Our Time: From World War II to Nixon, What Happened and Why* (New York: Vintage, 1976), 357.

27. *New York Times*, February 9, 1968, 1.

28. *Public Papers of the Presidents: Johnson 1968–69*, I (Washington, DC: Government Printing Office, 1970), 406–13.

29. *Public Papers of the Presidents: Johnson 1968–69*, I: 413–15.

30. "Meeting Between the President and Ambassador Bui Diem," March 19, 1968, NSF: Memos to the President, Rostow, Box 31, LBJL.

31. Senator Gravel Edition, *The Pentagon Papers*, IV:589–91.

32. Clifford, Oral History, LBJL.

33. Rostow to Johnson, March 25, 1968, NSF: NSC Histories, March 31st Speech, Box 49, LBJL.

34. Senator Gravel Edition, *The Pentagon Papers*, IV:592; Ridgway, "Meeting of So-Called 'Wisemen' on Viet-Nam, March 25–26, 1968," Gibbons Papers, Box 36, LBJL.

35. Summary of Notes, March 26, 1968, LBJ Papers, Meeting Notes File, Box 2, LBJL; see also Johnson to the President, March 27, 1968, President's Appointment File, Box 93, LBJL.

36. PBS, *Vietnam: A Television History*, "Tet, 1968."

37. Summary of Notes, March 26, 1968, and Summary, March 26, 1968, Johnson Papers, Meeting Notes File, Box 2, LBJL.

38. Summary, March 26, 1968, Johnson Papers, Meeting Notes File, Box 2, LBJL.

39. Ridgway, "Meeting of So-Called 'Wisemen' on Viet-Nam, March 25–26, 1968," Gibbons Papers, Box 36, LBJL.

40. PBS, *Vietnam: A Television History*, "Tet, 1968."

41. PBS, *Vietnam: A Television History*, "Tet, 1968."

42. Clifford, Oral History, LBJL.

43. PBS, *Vietnam: A Television History*, "Tet, 1968."

44. McPherson, Oral History, LBJL; Clifford, Oral History, LBJL.

45. Rusk to Johnson, March 25, 1968, NSF: NSC Histories, March 31st Speech, Box 48, LBJL; Clifford, Oral History, LBJL; McPherson, Oral History, LBJL.

46. 583rd NSC Meeting, March 27, 1968, NSF: NSC Histories, March 31st Speech, Box 49, LBJL.

47. Senator Gravel Edition, *The Pentagon Papers*, IV: 593–94.

48. *Public Papers of the Presidents: Johnson 1968–69*, I: 469–76.

49. *Public Papers of the Presidents: Johnson 1968–69*, I: 469–76.

50. *Public Papers of the Presidents: Johnson 1968–69*, I: 469–76.

51. Hodgson, *America in Our Time*, 361.

Chapter Five

THE MEANING OF TET

THERE IS NO DOUBT THAT THE TET OFFENSIVE WAS A decisive moment in the Vietnam War leading to the capping of American escalation of the war, a partial bombing halt, the first negotiations, and President Johnson's decision not to seek reelection. Why Johnson took these steps, however, has stirred a great deal of controversy. There are two, interrelated myths surrounding the Tet Offensive that supporters of the war use in defense of the U.S. intervention in Vietnam. The first is that a resounding American military victory in Vietnam was turned into defeat due to the political and psychological impact of the attacks in the United States. The cause of that defeat, and the second myth, was that the media, and television in particular, presented such a distorted picture of the attacks on the cities that it appeared that the war was being lost. This, in turn, led to a panic by the American public, and in parts of the Johnson administration, that led American officials to misunderstand the meaning of the attack and overreact to it. The result was the unnecessary beginning of the process of American withdrawal.

Both of these claims are false. While the Tet Offensive was certainly a surprise to the American people and government officials alike, in its timing, size, and place, it did not produce a dramatic swing in popular opinion. Support for the war had been eroding for the past year, and the Tet Offensive only continued that trend as the American objectives and national interest in Vietnam became more unclear all the time. Despite the claims of a military victory, the outcome of the battles was not clear, and it appeared to more and more people that it was a stalemate. Moreover, officials in the Johnson administration questioned the interpretation of the Tet Offensive as a victory and began to consider other options rather than the tried and failed continuation of American escalation.

Don Oberdorfer, in his study of the Tet Offensive based on his own reporting during the war and interviews, first raised the question of the media's coverage of Tet in 1971. Given the growth of television news viewership in the 1960s, he argued that "the television reflection of events was an important factor in the swing of public sentiment" away from supporting the war to opposing it.[1] The images broadcast of fighting in the American embassy, the streets of Saigon and Hue, and at Khe Sanh, he claimed, created an appearance of defeat and an unwinnable war. Moreover, "the pictures tended to agree with the dominant opinion of the correspondents and their editors at home—that the war was a stalemate and a mistake."[2] Oberdorfer, and others later, pointed to the fact that during the confusion surrounding the fighting on the grounds of the U.S. Embassy in Saigon, some reports erroneously claimed that the NLF sappers had taken the embassy building, thereby creating an impression that the NLF achieved more than it actually did.[3] That this incorrect information, as Oberdorfer notes, originated with American officials, that most reports did not include this statement, and that those news outlets that did carry this report quickly corrected their stories, has been ignored by those who picked up his claim that television played a decisive role in the understanding of the Tet Offensive and the outcome of the war. In addition, daily polling showed a "sudden jump in public hawkishness"[4] in the days immediately following the outset of the offensive, demonstrating further that the television images of the fighting did not turn the public against the war. This television thesis, nonetheless, became the standard explanation for many administration officials and other supporters of the war for the American failure in Vietnam.

The same year that Oberdorfer's book on Tet appeared, Lyndon Johnson published his memoirs. He asserted that the Tet Offensive was "a military defeat of massive proportions for the North Vietnamese and the Viet Cong" that failed to achieve their objectives of creating a massive uprising and destroying the Saigon government. "But the defeat the Communists suffered did not have the telling effect it should have had largely because of what we did to ourselves." Specifically, Johnson claimed that "there was a great deal of emotional and exaggerated reporting of the Tet offensive in our press and on television," and that the coverage of the fighting, what he termed a "chorus of defeatism," represented a "daily barrage of bleakness and near panic" that led the American people to "begin to think that we must have suffered a defeat" and to turn against the war. He stated that he was not surprised that certain opponents of the war reacted as they did, but the response of the Wise Men caught him off guard. Johnson "was surprised and disappointed that the enemy's effort produced such a dismal effect on various people inside government and others outside whom I had always regarded as staunch and unflappable."[5]

General Westmoreland leveled similar charges, claiming that critical reporting of the fighting by television reporters, who did not understand the true nature of the war, served the purposes of the enemy by portraying Tet as a crisis and defeat. This undercut support for the war at home and led the Johnson administration to miss the chance for victory.[6] A survey of the commanding generals who served in Vietnam found they all were critical of the television coverage, and held it responsible for declining support because it, they claimed, created the perception that the United States had suffered a defeat during the Tet Offensive and was losing the war.[7]

The most complete statement of the television thesis was made in 1981 by the journalist Robert Elegant who served as a reporter in Vietnam during the war. He claimed that "for the first time in modern history, the outcome of a war was determined, not on the battlefield but on the printed page and, above all, on the television screen." In retrospect, he stated, the United States had won the Tet Offensive and the military struggle. It had "virtually crushed the Vietcong in the South." Yet the war was lost because of "skewed reporting" that was "superficial and biased" and depicted the urban battles as a defeat. The reporters' antiwar sentiments, shock at the Tet Offensive, and "conviction of American guilt" led to an immediate interpretation of an National Liberation Front (NLF) victory that "resisted all the evidence pointing to a much more complex reality." Thus, "political pressures built up by the media had made it quite impossible" for the United States to continue the war at previous levels as the Johnson administration was pressured to reject further escalation leading to the eventual withdrawal of American forces and the loss of Saigon.[8] Others picked up on Elegant's attack on the media. For example, Keyes Beech, a journalist with a long career covering Asia, charged that "the media helped lose the war" due to its inaccurate reporting that swayed public opinion against the American effort in Vietnam. "What often seems to be forgotten," he wrote, "is that the war was lost in the U.S., not in Vietnam."[9]

Peter Braestrup's *Big Story*, a two-volume examination of press and television coverage of the Tet Offensive, is the most-cited work on this question. Braestrup concluded that the reporting on the attacks, particularly on the embassy in Saigon, was inaccurate at the outset, misinformed, and superficial. In the process, he claims, reporters overstated the shock created by the assault on the cities by focusing on the most dramatic events such as the battle on the embassy grounds and General Nguyen Ngoc Loan's assassination of an NLF prisoner on the street in Saigon. These reports created a misunderstanding of the significance of the fighting. Moreover, the narrow focus of the news coverage on the fighting in Saigon, Hue, and Khe Sanh created the misperception that the Tet Offensive was a victory for the NLF and North Vietnamese Army (NVA) and a defeat for American forces and Saigon. Unlike Elegant and Keyes, Braestrup cited inexperience and lack of understanding of the nature of the fighting, rather than ideology, to explain this development. "The inescapable conclusion," he argued, "even before Tet made it obvious, is that the U.S. major media, rich as they were in the 1960s, devoted insufficient resources and insufficient critical attention to the conflict." Thus, they did not understand the type of war being fought in Vietnam and were unprepared for an offensive the scale of Tet. This led to distorted coverage in the early days of the fighting and a sense that the United States had suffered a significant defeat.[10]

Still, as Braestrup has acknowledged, "no empirical data exist to link news coverage with changes in public opinion."[11] A number of other scholars, most notably George Donelson Moss, Chester Pach, William Hammond, and Daniel Hallin, have demonstrated that there is no evidence to support the charge that television reporting had a negative impact on public opinion or the outcome of the war. As Moss notes, "the quite remarkable fact about this widely held and deeply believed theory of television's impact on the outcome of the Vietnam war is that it is spurious. . . . All available data challenge the idea that television coverage was a decisive cause of the American failure in Vietnam." Rather, "television news became a scapegoat" in certain quarters for the loss of the war by those who could not admit the mistakes of American policy.[12]

Pach concurs, noting that one cannot know whether television news commanded the attention of the public or not, and that its effects on viewers "are almost impossible to determine with precision." Moreover, as Pach demonstrates through his content analysis of television's reporting on the Tet Offensive, it was not sensational or distorted. On the contrary, the "reports were perceptive and informative. They were also unsettling, both for the viewers who had become accustomed to the misleading optimism" stemming from the administration's fall 1967 public relations campaign "and for top government officials, who recognized the damage to their credibility." Thus, if the coverage of Tet had any impact, it was to expose the credibility gap between the claims of 1967 that the United States was winning the war and military stalemate on the ground, an interpretation of the events that many administration officials readily admitted to themselves.[13] Hammond reached a similar conclusion in his study of the military and the media in

Vietnam. While "news coverage of the Tet offensive had little effect on American public opinion, it served nevertheless
to reinforce the doubts that had surfaced within the Johnson administration during the previous year."[14]

Hallin's examination of the media and the war shows
that it was only when a significant number of American officials began to disagree about the meaning of Tet and the
necessity or benefits of further escalation that the war
moved into the "sphere of legitimate controversy." As a result, reporters, who had up until Tet rarely questioned the
administration's rationale for the fighting or evaluation of
the war, now presented different views and a range of opinions. This reporting provided greater legitimacy to critics'
views, but did not mark a turning point or a "shattered
American morale at home." Instead, Tet was "a crossover
point, a moment when trends that had been in motion for
some time reached a balance and began to tip the other
way."[15] As public opinion polls showed, support for the war,
which had been slipping throughout 1967, stabilized in the
wake of the administration's public relations campaign that
fall. With the Tet Offensive, there was an initial rallying to
the flag and then the trend of declining support and growing opposition returned.

What is most important to note about the press coverage of the Tet Offensive is that it was not a factor in the
decisive decisions made by the Johnson administration after
Tet. Senior officials in the Johnson administration were not
directly influenced by public opinion and certainly not by
television's coverage of the war. Rather, a crucial segment of
American officials and establishment figures, most notably
Clark Clifford and the majority of the Wise Men, came to
believe, based on the reports they received and their own
calculations, that Tet was not a victory in any meaningful

sense of the word and that the United States was stuck in a stalemate. The standard measures used up until then to measure progress—body counts, villages pacified, and enemy recruitment—were not only inaccurate, they concluded, but of little value in determining the course of the war. It was certainly true that the communist forces had suffered enormous casualties and had paid a high price for attacking the cities. But, officials now asked, what did these statistics mean in terms of making South Vietnam more secure, increasing the legitimacy of the Saigon government, or ending the fighting? What was the outcome of the Tet Offensive in terms of how much longer the United States would be at war in Vietnam and at what costs? Had any progress actually been made since 1965?

In asking these types of questions, Clifford, McGeorge Bundy, Dean Acheson, and others were influenced by the reports they received from the State Department, the CIA, and the Department of Defense, as well as by their contacts in the business and legal communities, the economic problems of the nation, and the growing unrest at home. Had they thought the war could still be won in a reasonable time frame and within reasonable costs, they would have supported further escalation. But after Tet, most officials in the Johnson administration, along with the Wise Men, could no longer see that as feasible. The evidence they received in February and March 1968 showed that due to the Tet Offensive the NLF was stronger and had gained greater control of the countryside, that the pacification program had collapsed, that the enemy had reserve strength and could match an American escalation, and that the Saigon government was weaker than a year earlier. No progress had been made in Vietnam since 1965. All that was achieved was a costly stalemate with no end in sight.

Thus the second myth, that the Tet Offensive was a military victory, is as incorrect as the television thesis. The Tet Offensive demonstrated that the United States could not win a limited war of attrition in Vietnam and had to change policy. In these terms, Tet was, in fact, a defeat. A defeat for the strategy of attrition and limited war in Vietnam, and for the strategy of using military power to force a political structure on Vietnam. This is certainly how the officials who prepared the materials for Clifford's task force saw it, how Clifford came to understand it, and why the Wise Men changed their position. And this is what Dean Acheson meant when he said the United States "can no longer do the job we set out to do in the time we have left and we must begin to take steps to disengage."[16] The war had proved more costly than any benefit the United States could achieve from continuing to escalate, and a wider war, including attacks on neighboring nations and North Vietnam, brought with it the danger of conflict with China and a global war. This was exactly what the policy of containment and limited war was supposed to prevent. The Clifford task force was the first strategic reassessment made since the decision to escalate in 1965, and it was this expert analysis that changed the course of the American war in Vietnam.

Given this new understanding, all of the previous assumptions about Vietnam that American policy had been based upon had to be reexamined. This, in turn, led to a cracking of the elite consensus on the necessity to continue the Vietnam War as key officials abandoned their previous support for the effort. Vietnam had only been important to the United States due to the logic of the Cold War. It was supposed to be a limited war that would demonstrate the resolve and credibility of American power and policy without leading to a direct conflict with either the Soviet Union or

China. It was also supposed to be a quick war whose costs would not disrupt the domestic economy or create division at home. The United States, however, had underestimated the power of Vietnamese nationalism and the indigenous nature of the war. By viewing Vietnam through the distorting lens of monolithic communism, American officials had misinterpreted the conflict as one of Northern aggression against the South and not as a revolutionary struggle that emerged in response to French colonialism.

Here was the dramatic change brought about by the Tet Offensive. It was not in public opinion. Rather, it was in the changing views of the establishment and the elite understanding of Vietnam that shifted in a short period of time away from support for the war and the necessity to continue escalation and led to Johnson's change of course. The majority of the Wise Men could no longer avoid the contradiction that the administration was claiming progress and victory after Tet and at the same time saying the situation was perilous and that further escalation at dramatic costs was necessary to succeed. As Clifford noted, this created "a great big swing all around from an almost unanimous belief in the rightness of our cause" by the Wise Men to the position "that we should not continue to pour blood and treasure into Viet Nam." The United States, they now concluded, had to find a road out because the war was not worth the damage it was causing at home and abroad.[17]

The new administration of President Richard Nixon, still seeking victory, would expand the war, covertly and overtly, into Cambodia and Laos in its effort to force Hanoi to capitulate to American terms and maintain a noncommunist government in Saigon. The result was four more years of fighting, increased domestic unrest, and deepening economic problems. But Nixon could not change the realities of the fighting or stave off the ever-growing pressure to deescalate the American commitment and withdraw from Vietnam. That point had been passed when the NLF and NVA launched their assault on the cities of South Vietnam in January 1968. Tet had made it clear that the war was a stalemate and that there would be no victory. American forces could create massive amounts of destruction and prevent a collapse of the Saigon regime, but they could not defeat the enemy at costs that were acceptable to American society. Johnson's March 31 decisions marked the beginning of the long, bloody, and painful process of disengaging from the Vietnam War.

The fighting would continue for the United States until 1973 when the Paris Peace Accords were signed and the last of American forces and POWs came home. Without the American props, the Saigon government could not stand against the communist forces and it fell on April 30, 1975, bringing a final end to fighting that had begun in 1945 and leaving an independent, united Vietnam under the rule of Hanoi. The Tet Offensive had been the decisive point on the road to that outcome. In the process, it also brought an end to the notion of an American Century. The consensus on containment was shattered, postwar prosperity had given way to stagflation and the ending of the Bretton Woods system, the credibility gap and distrust of the government continued to grow, and all American institutions were now being questioned at home. Tet had opened the door to new questions, attitudes, and answers about the war in Vietnam and America's role in the world.

NOTES

1. Don Oberdorfer, *TET!* (New York: Avon Books, 1971), 258–59.

2. Oberdorfer, *TET!*, 178.

3. Oberdorfer, *TET!*, 44–50.

4. Oberdorfer, *TET!*, 176.

5. Lyndon Johnson, *The Vantage Point: Perspectives of the Presidency, 1963–1969* (New York: Holt, Rinehart and Winston, 1971), 383–84.

6. William Westmoreland, *A Soldier Reports* (New York: Doubleday, 1976), 556–58.

7. Douglas Kinnard, *The War Managers* (Hanover, NH: University Press of New England, 1977), 89.

8. Robert Elegant, "How to Lose a War: Reflections of a Foreign Correspondent," *Encounter* (August 1981), 73–77.

9. Keyes Beech, "How to Lose a War: A Response from an 'Old Asia Hand,'" in Harrison Salisbury, ed., *Vietnam Reconsidered* (New York: Harper & Row, 1984), 152.

10. Peter Braestrup, *Big Story: How the American Press and Television Reported and Interpreted the Crisis of Tet 1968 in Vietnam and Washington* (Garden City: Anchor Press, 1978), 47.

11. Peter Braestrup, "The Tet Offensive–Another Press Controversy: II," in Harrison Salisbury, ed., *Vietnam Reconsidered* (New York: Harper & Row, 1984), 170.

12. George Donelson Moss, "News or Nemesis: Did Television Lose the Vietnam War," in George Donelson Moss, *A Vietnam Reader: Sources and Essays* (Englewood Cliffs: Prentice Hall, 1991), 249, 247.

13. Chester Pach, "Tet on TV: U.S. Nightly News Reporting and Presidential Policy Making," in Carole Fink et al., *1968: The*

World Transformed (New York: Cambridge University Press, 1998), 79–81.

14. William M. Hammond, *Public Affairs: The Military and the Media, 1962–1968* (Washington, DC: Center of Military History, United States Army, 1988), 372.

15. Daniel Hallin, *The "Uncensored War:" The Media and Vietnam* (New York: Oxford University Press, 1986), 168–78.

16. Summary of Notes, March 26, 1968, Johnson Papers, Meeting Notes File, Box 2, LBJL.

17. Clifford, Oral History, LBJL.

Bibliographic Essay

THE PAPERS AT THE LYNDON B. JOHNSON PRESIDENTIAL Library, Austin, Texas, are the essential starting point for understanding American policy and the Tet Offensive. The most important records are Presidential Papers of Lyndon B. Johnson that include the National Security File (NSF); National Security Council Histories; NSF: Country File, Vietnam; NSF: Memos to the President; NSF: National Security Council Meetings; NSF: Files of McGeorge Bundy; NSF: Files of Walt W. Rostow; Meeting Notes File; White House Central Files; Congressional Briefings on Vietnam File; Cabinet Papers; and the President's Appointment File (Diary Backup). Other important collections at the Johnson Library include the Papers of George Ball; Papers of Clark M. Clifford; Papers of William Gibbons; Papers of William C. Westmoreland; and the oral histories conducted with various members of the Johnson administration.

Significant published primary document collections include the Senator Gravel Edition, *The Pentagon Papers: The Defense Department History of United States Decisionmaking on Vietnam,* 4 volumes (Boston: Beacon Press, 1971); Department of

State, *Foreign Relations of the United States* (Washington, DC: Government Printing Office); *Public Papers of the Presidents: Lyndon B. Johnson* (Washington, DC: Government Printing Office, 1965–1970); *Executive Sessions of the Senate Foreign Relations Committee: Historical Series* (Washington, DC: Government Printing Office); and William C. Gibbons, *The U.S. Government and the Vietnam War: Executive and Legislative Roles and Relationships, Part IV: July 1965–January 1968* (Princeton: Princeton University Press, 1995). Important documents can also be found in Steven Cohen, ed., *Vietnam: Anthology and Guide to A Television History* (New York: Knopf, 1983); Marvin Gettleman, Jane Franklin, Marilyn B. Young, and H. Bruce Franklin, eds., *Vietnam and America: The Most Comprehensive Documented History of the Vietnam War* (New York: Grove Press, 1995); Gareth Porter, ed., *Vietnam: The Definitive Documentation of Human Decisions*, 2 volumes (New York: New American Library, 1979); and William Appleman Williams, Thomas McCormick, Lloyd Gardner, and Walter LaFeber, eds., *America in Vietnam: A Documentary History* (Garden City: Doubleday, 1985).

On the Tet Offensive, Don Oberdorfer, *TET!* (New York: Avon Books, 1971) provides an excellent journalistic account. *The Tet Offensive*, Marc J. Gilbert and William Head, eds. (Westport, CT: Praeger, 1996), is a first-rate collection of articles on various aspects of the event. Ronnie E. Ford, *Tet 1968: Understanding the Surprise* (London: Frank Cass, 1995), and James J. Wirtz, *The Tet Offensive: Intelligence Failure in War* (Ithaca: Cornell University Press, 1991), examine the question of why the Tet Offensive was such a surprise to American leaders. David Maraniss, *They Marched into Sunlight: War and Peace, Vietnam and America, October 1967* (New York: Simon & Schuster, 2003), analyzes the war prior to Tet, while Ronald H. Specter, *After Tet: The Bloodiest Year in Vietnam* (New York: Free Press, 1993), examines the war in the year following the Tet Offensive. Video footage on Tet can be found in "The Tet Offensive," *The Vietnam War with Walter Cronkite* (New York: CBS Video Library, 1985); and "Tet, 1968," PBS, *Vietnam: A Television History* (Boston: WGHB, 1985).

For broader studies of the Vietnam War that include chapters on the Tet Offensive, see Larry H. Addington, *America's War in Vietnam: A Short Narrative History* (Bloomington: Indiana University Press, 2000); Larry Berman, *Lyndon Johnson's War: The Road to Stalemate in Vietnam* (New York: Norton, 1989); Frances Fitzgerald, *Fire in the Lake: The Vietnamese and the Americans in Vietnam* (Boston: Little, Brown, 1972); James William Gibson, *The Perfect War: The War We Couldn't Lose and How We Did It* (New York: Vintage, 1986); George Herring, *America's Longest War: The United States and Vietnam, 1950–1975*, 3rd ed. (New York: Knopf, 1996); Stanley Karnow, *Vietnam: A History* (New York: Penguin, 1991); A. J. Langguth, *Our Vietnam: The War, 1954–1975* (New York: Simon & Schuster, 2000); Robert Mann, *A Grand Delusion: America's Descent into Vietnam* (New York: Basic Books, 2001); George Donelson Moss, *Vietnam: An American Ordeal*, 3rd ed. (Upper Saddle River, NJ: Prentice Hall, 1998); Robert D. Schulzinger, *A Time for War: The United States and Vietnam, 1941–1975* (New York: Oxford University Press, 1997); and Marilyn B. Young, *The Vietnam Wars, 1945–1990* (New York: Harper-Collins, 1991).

In addition to the works cited earlier, military aspects of the Tet Offensive are examined in Robert Buzzanco, *Masters of War: Military Dissent in the Vietnam Era* (New York: Cambridge University Press, 1996); Clark Clifford, "A Viet Nam Reappraisal," *Foreign Affairs*, vol. 47, no. 4 (July 1969); Douglas Kinnard, *The War Managers* (Hanover, NH: University Press of New England, 1977); Ngo Vinh Long, "The Tet Offensive and Its Aftermath," *Indochina Newsletter*, Nos. 49,

50, 51; and Edward Moise, "Why Westmoreland Gave Up," *Pacific Affairs*, vol. 58, no. 4 (Winter 1985–86). For the impact of bombing in Vietnam, see Mark Clodfelter, *The Limits of Air Power: The American Bombing of North Vietnam* (New York: Free Press, 1989); and Robert Anthony Pape, *Bombing to Win: Air Power and Coercion in War* (Ithaca: Cornell University Press, 1996).

Books on the year 1968 that have chapters on the Tet Offensive include Charles Kaiser, *1968 in America: Music, Politics, Chaos, Counterculture, and the Shaping of a Generation* (New York: Weidenfeld & Nicolson, 1988); Mark Kurlansky, *1968: The Year That Rocked the World* (New York: Ballantine, 2004); Irwin Unger and Debi Unger, *Turning Point: 1968* (New York: Charles Scribner's Sons, 1988); and Jules Witcover, *The Year the Dream Died: Revisiting 1968 in America* (New York: Warner Books, 1997).

Useful memoirs by leading participants include Clark Clifford with Richard Holbrooke, *Counsel to the President: A Memoir* (New York: Random House, 1991); Townsend Hoopes, *The Limits of Intervention* (New York: Norton, 1987); Lyndon B. Johnson, *The Vantage Point: Perspectives on the Presidency, 1963–1969* (New York: Holt, Rinehart and Winston, 1971); Robert McNamara with Brian VanDeMark, *In Retrospect: The Tragedy and Lessons of Vietnam* (New York: Times Books, 1995); Dean Rusk, as told to Richard Rusk, *As I Saw It* (New York: Norton, 1990); and William C. Westmoreland, *A Soldier Reports* (New York: Doubleday, 1976). On McGeorge Bundy, see Kai Bird, *The Color of Truth: McGeorge Bundy and William Bundy: Brothers in Arms* (New York: Simon & Schuster, 1998). Thomas W. Zeiler, *Dean Rusk: Defending the American Mission Abroad* (Wilmington, DE: Scholarly Resources, 2000), is essential for understanding Secretary of State Dean Rusk.

The antiwar movement and public opinion are examined in Terry Anderson, *The Movement and the Sixties* (New York: Oxford University Press, 1995); Charles DeBenedetti with Charles Chatfield, *An American Ordeal: The Antiwar Movement of the Vietnam Era* (Syracuse: Syracuse University Press, 1990); George Gallup, *The Gallup Poll: Public Opinion 1935–1971* Volume III (New York: Random House, 1971); *Gallup Opinion Index, Report No. 33* (Princeton: Gallup International, 1968); *Gallup Opinion Index, No. 35* (Princeton: Gallup International, 1968); Godfrey Hodgson, *America in Our Time: From World War II to Nixon, What Happened and Why* (New York: Vintage, 1976); David W. Levy, *The Debate Over Vietnam* (Baltimore: Johns Hopkins University Press, 1991); Melvin Small, *Johnson, Nixon, and the Doves* (New Brunswick: Rutgers University Press, 1989); *Antiwarriors: The Vietnam War and the Battle for America's Hearts and Minds* (Wilmington, DE: Scholarly Resources, 2002); Robert R. Tomes, *Apocalypse Then: American Intellectuals and the Vietnam War, 1954–1975* (New York: New York University Press, 1998); Tom Wells, *The War Within: America's Battle Over Vietnam* (Berkeley: University of California Press, 1994). See Anthony S. Campagna, *The Economic Consequences of the Vietnam War* (New York: Praeger, 1991), on the economic impact of the Vietnam War on the United States.

For critical accounts of the role of the media during Tet, see Peter Braestrup, *Big Story: How the American Press and Television Reported and Interpreted the Crisis of Tet 1968 in Vietnam and Washington* (Garden City, NY: Anchor Press, 1978), and "The Tet Offensive—Another Press Controversy: II," in Harrison Salisbury, ed., *Vietnam Reconsidered* (New York: Harper & Row, 1984); Keyes Beech, "How to Lose a War: A Response from an 'Old Asia Hand,'" in Salisbury, *Vietnam Reconsidered*; and Roger Elegant, "How to Lose a War: Reflections of a

Foreign Correspondent," *Encounter* (August 1981). More balanced studies are Daniel Hallin, *The "Uncensored War": The Media and Vietnam* (New York: Oxford University Press, 1986); William M. Hammond, *Public Affairs: the Military and the Media, 1962–1968* (Washington, DC: Center of Military History, United States Army, 1988); George Donelson Moss, "News or Nemesis: Did Television Lose the Vietnam War," in George Donelson Moss, *A Vietnam Reader: Sources and Essays* (Englewood Cliffs, NJ: Prentice Hall, 1991); and Chester Pach, "Tet on TV: U.S. Nightly News Reporting and Presidential Policy Making," in Caroline Fink et al., *1968: The World Transformed* (New York: Cambridge University Press, 1998).

INDEX

ABOUT THE AUTHOR

DAVID F. SCHMITZ IS THE ROBERT ALLEN SKOTHEIM Chair of History at Whitman College. He is the author of *Henry L. Stimson: The First Wise Man*; *Thank God They're On Our Side: The United States and Right-Wing Dictatorships, 1921–1965*; and *The United States and Fascist Italy, 1922–1940*.